GEORGI
and Friends

Georgi & Friends
Copyright © 2023 by Glynn

All rights reserved.

No part of this book may be reproduced in any form or by any electronic or mechanical means, including information storage and retrieval systems, without written permission from the author, except for the use of brief quotations in a book review.

For information contact :
(info@georgiandfriends.com)
http://www.georgiandfriends.com

First Edition: July 2023

BY GLYNN

GEORGI
and Friends

CONTENTS

Georgi and Friends: Free Fun for Kids of All Ages	vii
Here are some additional benefits of colouring:	ix
Chapter One	1
Landon	
Chapter Two	17
The Visitor	
Chapter Three	33
Testing Mole's Latest Invention	
Chapter Four	43
It's A Rat Race	
Chapter Five	59
Feeding Pete the Pelican?	
Chapter Six	75
Kidnapped	
Chapter Seven	95
Mikey's New Invention	
Chapter Eight	113
The Map	
Chapter Nine	133
Siruss	
Chapter Ten	151
Finding the Crown?	
Chapter Eleven	159
What Lies Below?	

Chapter Twelve 171
  Freedom for Siruss?
About Author 187

Georgi and Friends: Free Fun for Kids of All Ages

Looking for a fun and educational activity for your kids? Look no further than Georgi and Friends! Our website offers a variety of free colouring pages that your kids can enjoy. All of our images are available in black and white, so they're perfect for kids of all ages.

Our colouring pages feature a variety of different characters and scenes, so there's something for everyone. Whether your kids love animals, princesses, or superheroes, we have a colouring page for them.

In addition to being fun, our colouring pages are also educational. They help kids develop their fine motor skills, hand-eye coordination, and creativity. They also help kids learn about different colours, shapes, and patterns.

So what are you waiting for? Start colouring today! Your kids will love it, and you'll love knowing that they're learning while they have fun.

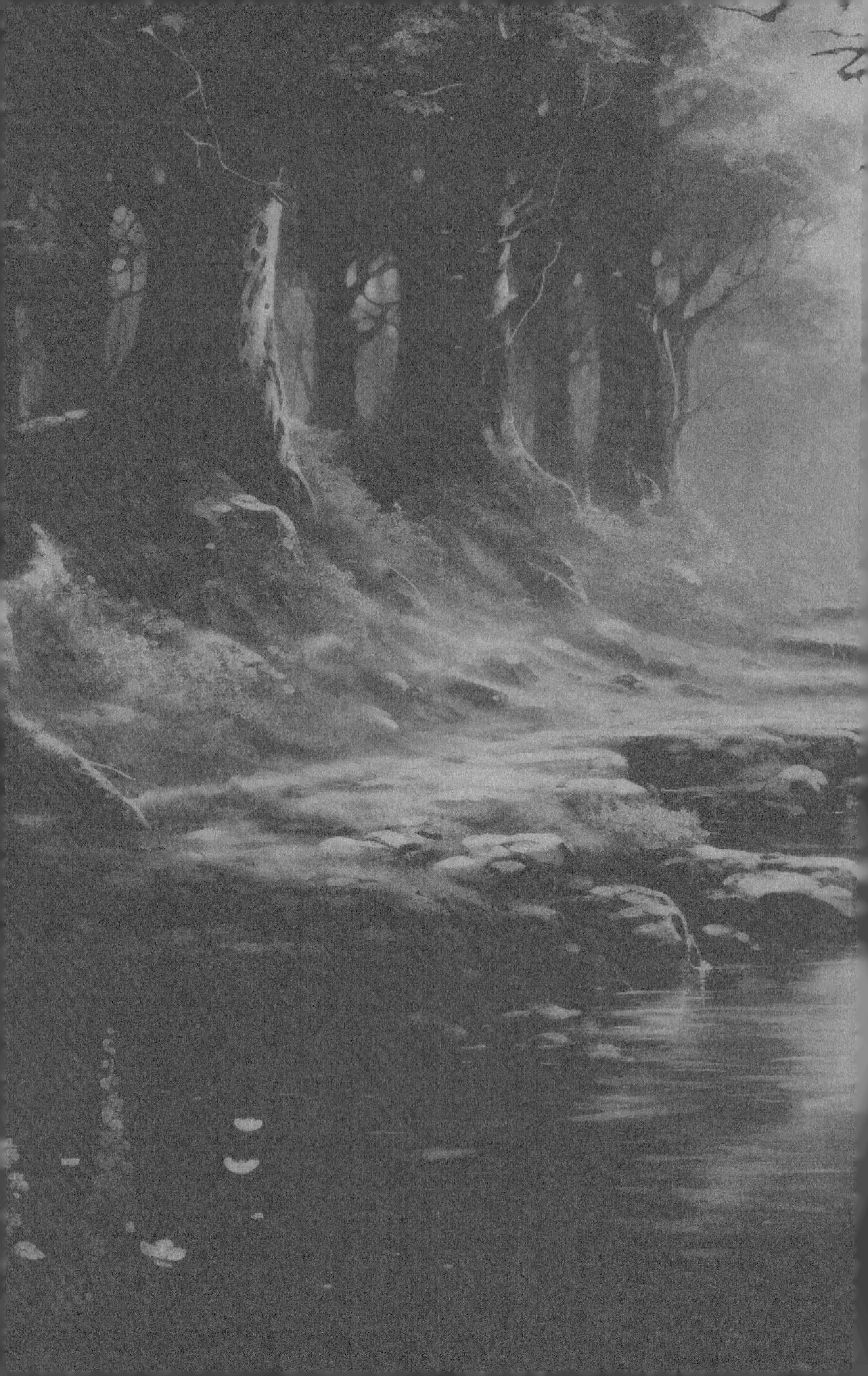

HERE ARE SOME ADDITIONAL BENEFITS OF COLOURING:

Colouring can help reduce stress and anxiety.
   It can help improve concentration and focus.
   It can help boost creativity and imagination.
   It can help improve fine motor skills.
   It can help kids learn about different colours, shapes, and patterns.
   So why not give Georgie and Friends a try? It's free, fun and educational!

   All of the images are freely available for downloaded in black and white for colouring at georgiandfriends.com

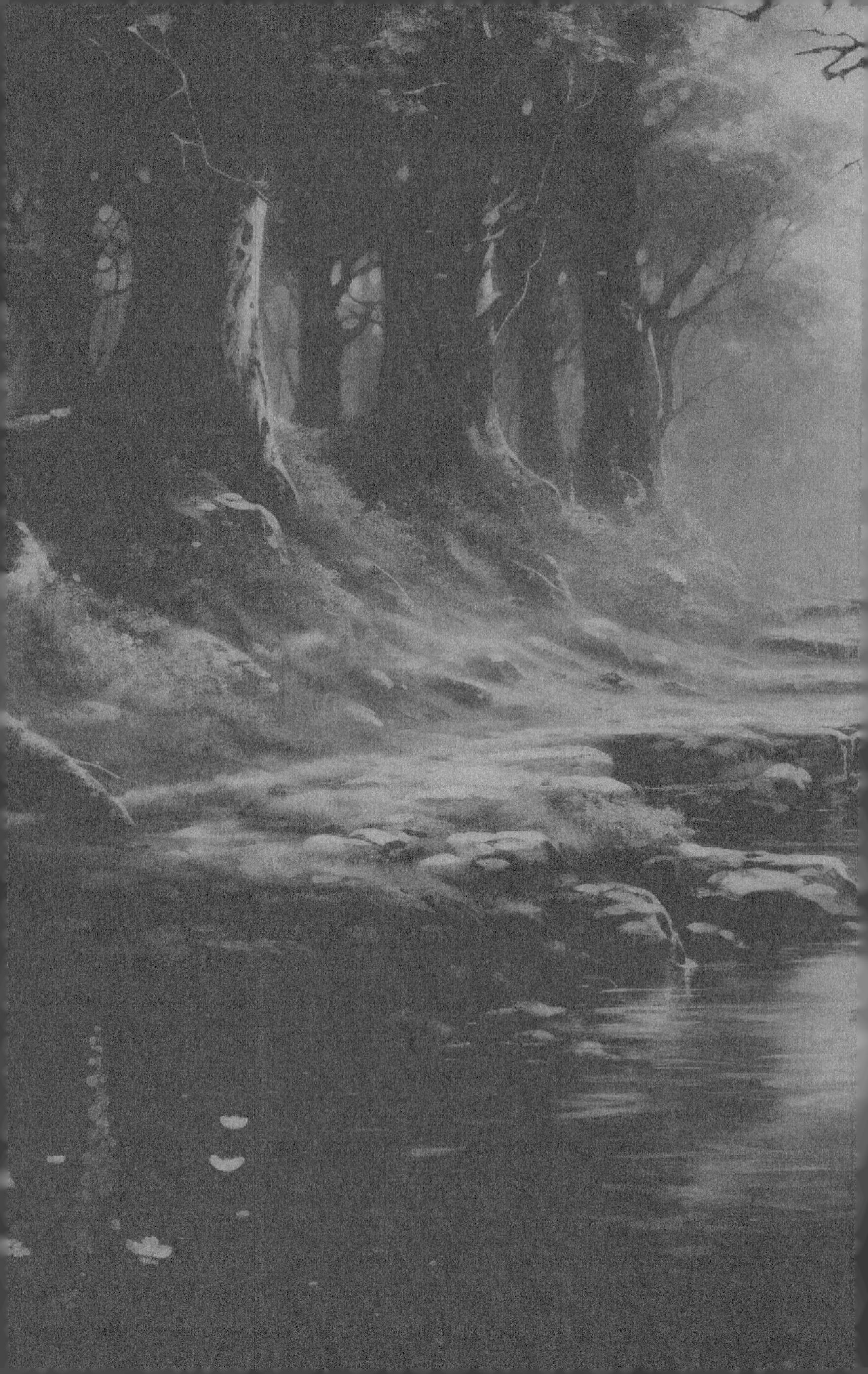

CHAPTER ONE

LANDON

It was a beautiful, fresh new day as Aussie Owl flew from the tree out over the Strawberry Fields which was next to his family nesting site.

He loved to feel the warmth of the summer breeze lifting his wings and the ease of which he could float effortlessly, as he drifted out over the lush green strawberry plants below.

In the distance Lady Frog was taking the children from the still lake in which they were playing, she was too focused on the children to notice the beauty and splendours of the reflection of the trees that have stood proud at the edge of the lake for many years.

Looking at the brilliance of the scrumptious red strawberries that he so much wanted to taste but did not have time to as he was on his way to meet his friend Georgi the Hedgehog.

Aussie and Georgi always met up with their friends and fellow gang members on the way to school, mainly to talk about their adventures after school.

Grandma Hedgehog, who lived at number 2 Strawberry Fields was always proud to say that she was a perfectly normal Grandmother who enjoyed looking after her young grandson Georgi while his parents were away.

Strawberry Fields is a wonderful, green leafy street located near a wild strawberry field pasture and on the edge of where a vast oak forest begins.

The strawberry plants grew as far as the eye could see until the start of the north side of the forest was seen on the horizon.

Most of the variety of animals and birds living in Landon live in or on the trees surrounding Strawberry fields.

At the bottom corner was a large lake inhabited by various fish and the homes of the local frog population of which a few attended the local school.

In the summer when most of the animals were not hibernating, the younger family members attended a local mixed school which was taught by an elderly Professor Badger.

With most of the birds having lessons, perched on branches in the trees in a class taught by Mrs. Owl.

Some of the more mature owls attended Professor Badgers class with the other older animals.

Grandma Hedgehog and Georgi occupied a reasonable sized dwelling in a hollowed out oak tree base, it consisted of 3 levels, the first of which was primarily for food preparation, the second was living and sleeping quarters and the upper level was used for storage.

Outside was a huge covered clearing where very little grew, because the large span of the oak tree blocked out too much of the sunlight.

Georgi always helped when Grandma needed it, picking cherries for Grandma to make pies. Helping clean the dishes and tidying the home on the numerous occasions when Georgi's friends visited to drink tea and eat Grandma's very popular cherry pie.

Grandma's cherry pie was world famous, at least world famous in this part of the world, in Landon.

Georgi was getting ready for the very short walk to meet his friends on the way to school, when Grandma said, "wait young man, let me check."

"Grandma I'm not a hoglet anymore" replied Georgi, using the standard name for a baby hedgehog. He stood proud in his red T shirt with white sleeves, red shorts and softly smiled.

"I understand young man, but this is what us Grandmothers do! We make sure, all is correct and as it should be!" she sweetly returned his smile, as she straightened Georgi's school bag on his shoulder, not even waiting until Georgi had finished tying the laces on his red and white trainers.

"Ok, Grandma, I will pick you some more cherries with my friends after school," he said, opening the front door to leave.

"You and your cherries, have a good day at school," she said with the broadest of grins.

"Have a good day also Grandma!"

Neither of them had noticed that it was raining outside and as Georgi walked beneath the spreading branches of the oak tree, his friend Alona Albino was waiting for him, as usual with her pink umbrella.

"Wait up Georgi!" she shouted as she moved towards Georgi with her umbrella, keen to stop her friend from getting wet.

"She has been there waiting for you, for about 10 minutes," stated Aussie Owl, knowing Alona was too far away to hear.

Aussie was another member of Georgi's Gang who had been sitting patiently on the tree branch waiting for Georgi to appear. "The early bird catches the worm; I don't know why I said that I'm an owl and I don't even like worms!" Said Aussie.

Georgi and Aussie had spoken about Alona many times before, Aussie always believed that Alona really liked Georgi and although he secretly wished that Aussie was correct in his assumption, he denied this every time the subject was mentioned.

Aussie was often correct and most of the time it was very annoying, but on this occasion, Georgi would be very happy for Aussie to be correct.

Alona was most unusual because she was completely white and being an Albino hedgehog, she had the most beautiful pink eyes you will ever see.

As she slowly walked towards them in her pink trainers with thin white stripes, Georgi was thinking how pretty she looked in her beautiful white dress with pink flowers.

Aussie flew up to Georgi," have you noticed how she always appears with an umbrella for you when it is raining, so you do not get wet?" he added, as he pushed his spectacles a little further back on his beak.

"Trust you about what?" Alona asked, hearing part of what Aussie said.

"We were talking about Mikey Mole wanting to join our gang," Georgi quickly butted in, hoping to spare an awkward conversation that might hurt Alona's feelings.

"Yes, trust me, his inventions never work right!" Aussie added swiftly, bringing the conversation away from the original and straightening his blue striped shirt.

"My umbrella works just fine, and Mikey made that for me!" Alona stated, not really understanding why letting him join the gang was such a big problem.

"But he didn't invent your umbrella, he made it from an existing design! I am talking about when he invented that cherry picker. The spring-loaded handheld machine that locked onto a branch and when it released, it came hurtling back towards us, knocking Mole and Georgi down, sending the rest of us diving for cover causing everyone to be showered by falling cherries!

"The cherry never falls far from the tree." Freddie added in amusement.

My mom is still trying to remove the red cherry stains from my shirt!" Aussie said annoyingly as he pulled his cap further down his head.

"Every morning for weeks now we have had this conversation about Mikey joining our gang and I think I finally have a plan to resolve this once and for all!"

"And what would that---" he stopped before finishing as Georgi indicated that Mikey was approaching.

Upon turning Aussie saw the blue dungaree clad figure rushing towards them.

"Hi guys, how are you all? So, what did you decide about me joining your gang?" he continued before anyone had a chance to answer.

"All good," Alona replied, smiling sweetly at Mikey. But at the same time Georgi also answered, "Good morning, Mikey, we are good and wish to address this issue. Every day when we meet you are now asking us the same question about joining our gang. You know we don't really need anyone else to join us, but…" he continued as he raised his hand towards Mikey to stop him interrupting.

"I have an idea about deciding this once and for all, then if you agree and we say no, that will be the end of it, Ok?" Mikey bowed his head and looked to the floor, "Ok," he replied, fearing the worst as he kicked a fallen acorn along the ground.

"I want to set you a task, pass this and you will be a welcome member of our gang, but first we need to meet with Freddy Frog together about this," said Georgi, feeling very happy about his idea being a win, win situation for all concerned.

"So, what are we waiting for, let's go speak with Freddy!" added Georgi triumphantly.

"What's this idea, then Georgi" Aussie asked curiously as they walked along the narrow winding path, next to those wonderfully inviting strawberries and headed towards the lake.

"All in good time!" George replied in a tone that Aussie knew he would have to wait and see just like everyone else then gradually his mind started thinking about his earlier plan, Strawberries.

"Let's stop and have some strawberries!" Aussie exclaimed, already tasting the sweet soft flesh in his mouth.

"Wait until we have settled this first and if we have time before school then ok," said Georgi thinking that celebrating with strawberries was a great idea, he started walking a little faster as they could see the shimmering blue lake in the distance.

"Don't worry Mikey" said Alona, seeing that he was very nervous about this. After all Alona understood that this was his dream to belong to be a part of something, to have fun with his friends. "It will all be ok, you'll see!" as she placed her hand on his shoulder a saw a smile began to form on his cheery face.

"I hope so!" Mikey replied, desperately trying to return Alona's smile as they moved from the canopy of the large oaks and into the radiant warm sunlight.

Suddenly there was a slurping sound from beside them. Georgi chuckled to himself as he saw a frog's long tongue come flying out from the strawberry plants and make a direct hit with Aussie's cap.

It all happened so quickly, one second you could hear the slurp, the next second Aussie's cap had disappeared. "What was that? What happened?" quickly followed by "where is my cap!"

By this time Georgi was laughing hysterically and although the others also started laughing, they didn't know why they were laughing!

"Good morning, Freddy!" Somehow, he managed to control his laughter. "Please give Aussie his cap back before he starts whining!" he added. "Freddy! Where? My cap, what's going on?"

Just as quickly as Aussie's cap had disappeared another slurp was heard and Aussie's cap was back on his head, not as it originally was but it had returned.

What just happened? Aussie asked the question again. Georgi explained that a frog has a long, elastic tongue that it uses to catch its food and that Freddy had just used his to remove and then quickly replace Aussie's cap.

Aussie was furious! "That was completely stupid and downright dangerous somebody could have been seriously injured!" he screamed as Freddy Frog stepped out from the strawberry plants by now laughing uncontrollably. "You should have seen your face Aussie, it was priceless!" Grinned the gang's resident prankster as he took out his sunglasses from the inside of his red waistcoat to give him some protection from the sun. "And if you had hit my eye instead, I could have fallen to the floor and damaged a leg or even worse, broken a leg!" Aussie replied, clearly not impressed as he adjusted his cap.

"Relax, I don't miss, I have been practicing this all my life, since I was knee high to a grasshopper!" he answered as he put his sunglasses on and smiled at everyone.

"Ok, enough you two, no damage was done, and we have more important things to discuss!" Georgi quickly snapped at Aussie and Freddie hoping to avoid any further arguments.

"Now as you all know for a while now, Mikey has been asking everyday if he can join us. He knows that we don't want any more members in our club, Georgi continued as all eyes fixed on Mikey. I suggest that Mikey creates something useful and if he does this then we should accept him in our gang. If he cannot then I am sorry" he briefly paused as he looked straight at Mikey, "but we really don't need another member!"

"Two wrongs don't make a right," said Aussie. We don't need something crazy like that cherry picker you invented, my mom is…" but Mikey Mole interrupted. "I think I have just the idea, but I will need a couple of days to complete it!" Mikey replied gleefully.

"So, we are all agreed?" asked Georgi.

Everyone replied with a resounding, "Yes!" except for Freddie who nodded and added, "I think this will be a very interesting event, don't you agree?" he said with a huge grin aimed at Aussie.

"It might be a good idea not to wear any good clothes during this event," he added as everyone except Aussie chuckled.

"All agreed," Georgi stated, still smiling. "Now let's go and eat some strawberries!"

This was met with cheers of agreement as they all patted Mikey on the back and wished him success with his task as they merrily headed towards the strawberries.

They walked to the regular place, which was not far from the school, it was a very small patch of ground with a scattering of brightly covered red mushrooms.

The biggest of the mushrooms they used as a table with the smaller ones nearby used as stools.

As Georgi and Freddy picked a large succulent, red strawberry and placed it on the mushroom table, Mikey took a saw from his tool belt and began to cut slices from it.

So, this is what you have made? Freddy asked, joking with Mikey.

"If only it was that simple" Mikey answered. "So, what are you going to make?" enquired Freddy.

"I am not going to say, I will take the next two days before and after school and you will see in a couple of days' time!" he replied confidently.

"That's the spirit! Added Alona, "I don't know what it is but I already feel it will be something great for our Treehouse!" she exclaimed with her magnificent smile.

"Actions speak louder than words," said Aussie. His mind was only focusing on strawberries, so much so, that he could almost taste the sweet squishiness with every cut that Mikey made. He wanted so much to feel that tasty texture in his mouth but had to wait until almost last!

As they set off there was a huge commotion coming from the direction of the school. Loud noises, lots of shouting, squealing and a very loud rumbling sound.

Their pace quickened until they were running towards the school, Georgi sent Aussie on ahead to see what the racket was about.

Aussie was flying towards the rats as the gang arrived at the school, "Rats Georgi, Rats attacked the school and now they are attacking Strawberry Fields!" screamed Aussie as he wondered if he was dreaming this or if it was real. But it was definitely real.

They saw some sort of machine moving quite quickly, it was covered in rats and creating immense damage and devastation to Strawberry Fields. Their machine was cutting down everything like a plague of locusts. They were breaking plants, wooden buildings, tables, and chairs went flying and then broke like twigs when they landed.

Amongst all the commotion they could hear the sounds of whoops of laughter, howling and cheers as this rat covered, car type, quickly turned in the distance.

"They are coming back!" screamed Aussie in full panic mode as he flew quickly towards his friends.

The rats were destroying everything in their path but quickly turned to run away when they noticed Professor Badger hurtling towards them. The rats quickly disappeared into the thorn bushes; Professor Badger realised that with the rats in the thorns chasing them was futile, so he quickly turned and headed back towards the school.

As they approached Professor Badger he beckoned Aussie to him, "Aussie, fly to my house as quickly as you can and tell Mrs. Badger that the rats have attacked Strawberry Fields and the school and instruct her to summon the Badger Battalion to meet me near the lake as quickly as possible!" he said his eyes filled with anger. The pupils had never seen Professor Badger in a rage like this before. "After that I want you to go to Harry Hedgehog's home and ask him to assemble all the animals he can muster to help with this mess!" he added as he angrily twisted his grey whiskers.

"Freddy and Alona, I want you to go to where the younger children are assembled, keep an eye on them and try to calm things down for me," he ordered.

Freddy and Alona turned, to follow his instructions, "Georgi and Mikey you are with me! With that, he started walking towards the devastation and the destruction of many strawberry plants next to the school.

It was terrible, the once dirt paths were now green covered with the leaves that had been hacked off the strawberry plants all mixed in with pieces of red strawberry scattered everywhere.

The school was also a mess, broken mushrooms needed to be removed and so many chunks of mushroom were strewn almost everywhere.

"Professor Sir, what happened here? Georgi asked. "Rats in some kind of machine attacked the school and the damaged plants that you see at the same time."

There were many younger rats sitting on something of theirs with sticks destroying everything in their path, regardless of what it was! He continued the anger clear in his voice.

Georgi, Mikey, and the Professor stopped and looked at the calamity they could see before them.

Many of the mushrooms within the school had been badly damaged, most of the strawberry plants that were in the rat's path had most of their leaves cut away and there were many with damaged fruit.

"Ok Mikey, I want you to start repairing these mushrooms, any damage needs covering somehow, the other animals will assist you with this when they arrive. Tell them to split into 2 groups, one going from the school to the left, where the rats originated and the other group to go straight ahead" he commanded as he put his paw above his eyes and shook his head in despair.

"For the mushrooms it is important to stop any elements getting into the plants and infecting them and hopefully this will help them to repair the damage done. The strawberries will grow back in a few weeks' time, they just need any debris like leaves removing, to help them grow."

"I can cover them with some of these strawberry leaves that have been hacked off", Mikey suggested.

"Good idea Mikey and any fruit that is on the floor but is still ok needs to be washed and taken to Georgi's Grandma's so she can do something with it!" "At least something tasty will come from this," he said with a smile that was quickly replaced with a grimace.

"Oh, and ask the first of the elders to arrive to escort the younger children to home."

"Why do they need escorting Professor? Mikey asked "I'm a little worried that those monstrous animals will return, and they will be better at home for the rest of today. It was a blessing that the children had only just started to arrive when it all started, it would have been terrible if this happened 10 minutes or so later when everyone was in lessons." He breathed a sigh of relief.

Professor Badger was correct, the only blessing from this was that the children were not yet in school.

"Ok Georgi you will accompany me seeing how you witnessed all of this vandalism! The Professor declared as they started to follow the path through the destruction.

As they started, they heard a loud rumbling in the distance in the direction that they were heading. "Don't worry about that, it is just the Badger Battalion on its way to meet us at the lake."

He said reassuringly.

"Now hopefully we can sort this out without too many problems!" "Just make sure that you stay close to me Georgi. Things could get a bit tricky, just you do exactly as I say, and all will be fine" he added.

"We are going to see his royal ratness King Khan the fourteenth and he better have some good answers, or it could be war! Now young Georgi I need you with me as an independent representative of Landon" and with that he told Georgi "You'll need to jump on my back and hold on tight to my jacket collar! It will be far quicker travelling this way" he said as he lifted the young hedgehog onto his back.

Then the Professor went down on all fours and ran like the wind, Georgi had never travelled this fast in his life, he realised as the strawberry plants went whizzing by.

Very quickly they were at the lake and Georgi saw 6 or 7 Badgers waiting patiently for them and these Badgers were huge, much larger, and younger than the Professor.

As they approached, they stood upright from their previously seated positions and moved to greet them both.

The Professor ordered one of them to wait for the remainder of the Battalion and whispered to him instructions he was to relay to the General.

The other 6 would accompany us immediately, with this we set off again at an amazing pace with the Professor leading this part of the Badger Battalion.

"Are you ok up there young man? He asked. "Fine Sir, it's an amazing view from up here," he added.

Georgi could see the vastness of the lake, which was surrounded by reeds for most of its part.

Occasionally, he glimpsed some large fish when they approached the surface, colourful birds standing at the edge drinking on this beautiful summer's day except for the earlier events.

Almost as quickly as he saw the lake it disappeared from his view as they entered Landon Woods, they still had much further to go but at this speed it would not be long before they were there.

Rat City was located very close to Manland and Georgi had never been to either place before or even met the Rat King, but he knew it would be a day that he would be telling stories about for many years to come.

As they hurtled through the lush green undergrowth Georgi cast a glimpse behind them, the others were closely following the Professor's lead.

The badger directly behind them gave Georgi a comforting smile but that didn't stop Georgi from wishing the whole battalion was already with them now.

"Will the rest of the battalion be far behind us Professor?" Georgi asked, hoping for a reassuring answer as he was completely unaware of what would transpire when they reached Rat City.

"Ah, don't worry Georgi they will only be 5 minutes or so behind us and I will be talking for much longer before anything happens! This isn't my first rodeo" He replied, "All will be ok, your Grandma will kill me if anything happens to you! He answered comfortingly with a chuckle in his voice.

After what seemed like a lifetime the Professor's pace slowed, they were entering the realms of Rat City.

The green undergrowth quickly disappeared and was replaced by piles of rubbish; the trees looked terrible with many of them missing their bark and covered in scratch marks.

It was like they were entering a world that was only in "black and white" everything was mainly grey or black. A dark, dank, dirty, smelly, horrible, gloomy place, which was completely opposite to Landon, Georgi wondered how anything could live there.

2 rat guards signalled for them to stop, the Professor slowed considerably and as he stopped almost as if they were not there, with a very quick left then right he sent both guards flying into the undergrowth.

He whispered further instructions to Georgi "ok I understand Professor" he answered confidently.

"Between me and you, I hate rats, very dirty creatures!" The Professor told him as they continued with their journey, their objective was still unknown to Georgi.

As they travelled just a little further Georgi could see a small group of about 20-30 rats directly in their path attempting to block their advance.

"Are you ready Georgi? The Professor asked. "Just say when!" He replied, as Georgi was now curled up in a ball on his shoulders.

"Now Georgi!" and with this command the Professor stopped suddenly hurling Georgi directly at the group of rats. He was hurtling towards them like a prickly cannon ball.

Georgi crashed into the rats, he could see nothing, only hear the rats screams and yelps against his spikey coat. Many were sent flying, others fled, and the remainder were flung into the undergrowth when the Professor arrived to retrieve Georgi.

"Are you ok Georgi? He asked. "I'm fine, is the coast all clear now?" "We are clear, rats gone, well done! Beautiful strike, I think you hit almost all of them and I managed to get the ones that you did not!" he said with a smile as he hoisted Georgi back onto his shoulders and they again set off.

"Almost there" the Professor continued, "so please stay close with these creatures anything can happen." He added angrily.

Georgi had no intention of doing anything other than what he instructed him, he planned to follow the Professor's instructions to the letter.

They were now deep inside Rat City as the Professor slowed dramatically almost to a walk.

Georgi started seeing more and more rats running along beside them, following them to their destination and he could help but notice how horrible this place smelled.

It had an aroma like nothing that Georgi had ever sensed before, a dirty, unhygienic smell surrounded them.

He wasn't sure whether it was the rats that were shadowing them or if it was just this place that smelled so bad.

"Stay alert guys," the Professor commanded as a rat who stood in their way was sent hurtling into the bushes by the Professor's left paw.

Very soon they reached a clearing, like a theatre, at the other end was a raised stage and many rats began scurrying to the front of this stage like they were trying to protect something but there was nothing there.

A gong was sounded many times as more and more rats headed towards the stage at the other end of the clearing. Hundreds appeared from nowhere lining up in between the Badgers and the stage as we slowly walked forward, and the other badgers moved to our left and right.

"Khan, where are you? Get out here now! You have some very important questions to answer! Where are you, Khan? Khan! The Professor bellowed.

Then there was a brief silence and all that could be heard was the whispering of the ever-increasing number of rats in front of them.

"Georgi I will tell you that whatever happens now you must remain quiet, at all times. It's going to be a little bit tense for a while now" he quietly whispered to Georgi as he acknowledged his request.

CHAPTER TWO

THE VISITOR

As more and more rats assembled everything suddenly went quiet the rats stopped whispering but kept their gaze firmly fixed on these unknown visitors.

"His Royal Ratness, King Khan the 104th" one of the rats announced to huge cheers from the gathering of rats was almost deafening.

A large old rat draped in a large cape walked across the stage to a throne in the centre.

He raised his hands in appreciation of the cheers he was receiving from his subjects, then all fell quiet as he lowered his arms and sat on his throne.

"And what brings you to Rat City, old badger? He asked as his long tail wrapped around a drinking glass and moved it to his mouth.

"You know very well why we are here; did you think you could send one of your raiding parties to attack us and that we would do nothing? He questioned angrily.

"We haven't dispatched any raiding parties since we signed the treaty with you a very long time ago!" The king answered looking quite bewildered.

Khan summoned one of his Generals to uncover what was happening as Professor Badger angrily twisted his whiskers impatiently waiting for his answer.

"So, you think to come here and start a war with us?" "If necessary," the Professor instantly answered as he glared angrily towards the king. "Please enlighten me, while I understand that you are much bigger and stronger than any rat in my command, do you really think that you can start this war and defeat my army of almost a thousand rats with just yourself, 6 badgers and 1 small hedgehog?" He questioned, as all the rats present laughed hysterically.

Many were repeating what Khan had said, "6 badgers and a small hedgehog!" as the laughter continued. "Enough" Shouted the King, the laughter slowly subsided.

"Do you really think that I would come here with just a small company of men?" Professor proclaimed. "What information do you have from our scouts?" Khan asked his General. "Sire we have had no information from our scouts since these arrived!" he informed the king awkwardly.

"In fact," he continued but Khan abruptly interrupted him "so where is your army?" he asked, thinking that the Professor was just trying to frighten him. "General Storm, will you and your men all move forward so we can all see you! He bellowed his command while smiling triumphantly at the King.

Khan looked very confused, until his General whispered to him, "we haven't had any contact whatsoever with our scouts, nothing at all, they have disappeared!"

At that same moment there was a huge rumbling as the Battalion advanced forward into plain view. A few of the rats closest to the approaching Badger soldiers took it upon themselves to attack but were not ever going to be any match against them.

They were swatted almost like flies or sent hurtling to the undergrowth. The Rat King ordered them to stand down but for most of them this order was too late as one of the last was sent flying towards Khan landing on the stage beside him.

"You were not given any orders to attack!!" He screamed at his soldier as he whipped him with his tail. Georgi looked on in amazement, he had never seen this many badgers in one place at any one time. Unable to count how many of them there were, he guessed it was somewhere between 80 and 100 very large badgers had just surrounded most of the city!

King Khan was visibly shaken by this surprising event, now he knew why he had not heard anything from his scouts.

The King's General, knowing that they were clearly outnumbered, spoke firstly to his king. "Sire, may I address the badgers as I now believe what the problem is and can resolve this before it gets out of hand. As the King nodded in agreement the General turned to face the badgers.

"I believe I understand the cause of this problem Professor, a week ago we expelled 18 rats from our City. They were criminals, very destructive vandals, good for nothing, who didn't want to follow our rules, our code. And since you state you were attacked by rats, and I can categorically inform you that it was nobody from here therefore it only leaves the rebels who could have attacked Landon."

"That is all well and good but how are you proposing to stop this?" Professor Badger insisted.

"I will send my best soldiers to capture these varmints and then we will decide what to do with them, agreed? There really is no need for all of this, let's keep our treaty intact?" He pleaded.

"And what will we do in the meantime until they are captured? Understand we have many youngsters that could have been seriously injured in this or even another attack." He answered apprehensively. "We will track them down and keep you informed of their whereabouts, until we bring them in then that way you will at least have an idea whether they are near or far away and if you can be of any assistance in their capture, it would be greatly appreciated." He boldly requested.

"I need to speak with my General, give me 5 minutes." Professor stated commandingly, followed by "Georgi, you're with me!" he said, summoning Georgi to him as he made his way to speak with General Storm. "What do you make of all this, General?" He asked, looking to him for guidance. "I think it makes complete sense to me, after all, it was only a small party and other than starting a war between us what was achieved by it, when nothing was taken. To avoid any bloodshed, I think we should give them enough time to locate and capture these animals and one of us should be party to any proceedings after they round them up." "I agree, it's the only thing that makes any sense and at least now they do know we can attack their City in large numbers very easily so that should make them aware that we can return again if this is not correct." Professor Badger added confidently.

"Ok Khan we agree, but with one condition?" Professor Badger added. "Which is?" asked the King, happy that a battle he couldn't win had been averted. "When you catch these rebels, we want our representatives to witness the trial and sanction the punishment! "And also understand that if this story is not correct, we will be back here in bigger numbers than today!" The Professor said knowing that he was putting the fear of death into a very scared King.

"As we speak my soldiers are already organizing a search party to find these outlaws" Khan stuttered clearly worried by the Badger threat.

'Then it's agreed, and it will be advisable to keep your soldiers away from Landon until this is resolved as I cannot guarantee their safety." He added making sure that the rats stayed in their own region and didn't come anywhere near us.

"Agreed and I will keep you informed of our progress and their location when we track them down!" Khan stated realizing the potential problem had been averted.

"Right then General Storm, Badger Battalion and Georgi, we will return to Landon and wait for news from you, but we will not wait long!" The Professor commanded as he lifted Georgi onto his shoulder for the journey back to Landon.

Georgi felt like the world had just been lifted off his shoulders as they left Rat City and he could finally see some colour, the green trees, shrubs and all the other things he was much more familiar and comfortable with.

The journey back was at a much slower pace. There wasn't a rush to reach our destination as there was before, but Georgi liked this as it gave him much more time to look around.

Soon the lake appeared again but this time there were many animals present enjoying the day without school and the summer sun.

Everyone stopped to look in awe as the Badger Battalion passed the still, clear, lake, that was a hive of activity. It was reminiscent of a big parade being led by Professor Badger and General Storm.

"So, what did you think of Rat City Georgi? The Professor asked curiously. "I thought it was a terrible place, how can anything live there and the smell, why do they live like that?" he said, answering him with another question. "They live that way simply because they are too lazy! You saw how many of them there were, they could easily organize into groups and make a great place for all of them to live in, they choose not to, just forage for food, and relax." He replied disappointingly. Georgi was sure the Professor wished he could change the rat's lifestyle, but unfortunately, he was powerless to do anything about that part of their lives.

Georgi felt great that he could finally see Strawberry Fields in the distance and was looking forward to Grandma's Cherry Pie which hopefully everyone else hadn't eaten by now.

All the earlier mess to the strawberries had now been cleared away and although they resembled a badly cut hedge everyone knew that in a few short days most of it would grow back although the fruit would take longer to reappear. The school was the worst looking place of all this with mushrooms covered in leaf bandages to help their recovery but only one or two had been completely removed and would grow back before much longer.

As they arrived at Georgi's Grandma's they could see much activity ahead, all the animals in Landon had prepared food for their returning heroes who thankfully didn't need to do anything other than discuss the situation with King Khan but nevertheless they were all hungry after their long journey.

Everyone started cheering as they got closer and Georgi felt very proud as he heard his friends shouting his name, even though he only attended as an observer.

Reaching their destination, the Professor slowly lowered Georgi to the ground amid much cheering and quietly told him, "enjoy the moment" with his Grandma rushing towards him.

"I am so happy you are ok and so proud of what you have done today, you're my little hero!" she said with tears of happiness in her eyes.

People were already starting to ask what had happened and the Professor said, "Let's eat and Georgi can then tell you all about it!" he answered with a huge, happy grin as he put his arm around Georgi and walked towards the food they had prepared.

"We have certainly earned Grandma Hedgehog's Cherry Pie today, isn't that right General?" He was already eating but nodded in agreement. "A strawberry a day keeps the doctor away," said Grandma.

After they had eaten and to very loud applause, the Professor, General and the rest of Badger Battalion, went to discuss the rest of the day's events and plan for any recurrence.

Georgi recapped the episode of the day and gave thanks to everyone who had helped with trying to get Landon back to normal, also to Grandma and her helpers for making a wonderful pie with green "Chayorchik" tea.

Everyone lifted their cups in a toast to Landon, Grandma, its people, and all said, "Chayorchik!"

They drank a toast, celebrating the wonderful people of the City of Landon. "Bless your hearts," said Grandma.

Georgi didn't realize it at the time, but he would be telling the story of this day hundreds of times for many years to come.

The Professor sent a message that the next day would be a holiday in celebration of this event and as the elders started to plan the following day Georgi and his gang plus Mikey Mole moved a short distance away from the main group. Everyone congratulated him again and there were many more questions about how he felt and what he would have done if a war had started.

"Enough questions for today." Georgi told the guys, "Let's go and eat some more Cherry Pie with green "Cha-yorchik" tea." They all smiled in agreement.

Grandma served them all a little more pie and Georgi suggested they go to their tree house the next day. But as they were discussing it Grandma added, "I sorry Georgi but you will need to be here for the celebrations because you were a part of this incident, you won't need to be here all day, but you will be expected for the speeches." She said, smiling at her hero.

"Ok," answered Georgi, we will go after this. Mikey declined much to everyone's amazement, but he wanted to work and finish his project.

Alona the "Umbrella girl" smiled and asked him "How is your project coming along?

"Excellent, better than I imagined" he smiled confidently. "Any information or hints you can tell us?" She asked hopefully. "No none, it's a surprise!" he replied. "I may finish it tomorrow with more time to work on it." He added confidently.

"So, it will be a good day all round," Georgi added. 'Now I need some sleep, big day tomorrow!"

"See you all in the morning, have a great evening! Everyone wished each other good night and then went to their homes, all very proud of their friend Georgi.

After all the celebrating and Georgi's speeches were finished the guys went off to their tree house while Mikey returned to his workshop to finish his project.

He had already agreed to meet the gang at the tree house tomorrow so he could present his completed task to them.

The conversation was now about what Mikey was doing, "I wonder what it could be?" Alona asked curiously, hoping that one of them had a clue what he was doing.

"I went past his and his Uncle's workshop on the way home the other day but couldn't get any idea as to what they were working on." Aussie replied, "So, you are spying on him now? Can you not simply wait until tomorrow?" Georgi asked. "I was simply passing and just tried to take a closer look, so it's not spying!" Aussie replied.

All the way there Georgi spoke about how much he had enjoyed his adventure with the Badger Battalion and that he wanted to enjoy many more quests with the gang.

At the tree house they all got comfortable, and Georgi told them all a story which was told to him when they were returning from Rat City.

He had been talking to the Professor about how dirty, smelly Rat City was and why anyone could live in conditions like that. The Professor had told him that it was because they were lazy, but that wasn't the complete story.

Many years ago, the Rats lived much differently from how they do today, their City was much closer to Landon then one day there was a very bad rainstorm which destroyed many of their dwellings.

The Rats started blaming each other and fighting broke out amongst themselves. The Rat King told everyone of his idea to take over Landon and they would all live there, so he sent his army to attack us while he remained safe in the City. Then there was a major disaster, the Rat King and the remaining population were destroyed or washed away, nobody really knows what happened, but the Rat City disappeared.

The Rat Army, completely unaware of their City's devastation, attacked Landon but this was also a disaster for the Rats. They were easily beaten back deep into the woods. The Badgers pushed them deeper and deeper until eventually they surrendered and now, they didn't even have a City to return to.

The treaty of Vermini was agreed, named in memory of the Rat King who had been lost with their homes. When this was signed, and the Rats built their new City where they are to this day, but something was missing. When Rhandor was King he had a Golden Crown, known as the Crown of Hairies and this was the sign of a true ruler, it gave him the respect of the Rat people, the command of the soldiers, all listened to every word that he commanded.

Today the King Khan although he is a direct descendant of the original Kings without the crown, he is just a figurehead a rat who gives orders, sometimes they obey his commands but most of the time they do not.

The Professor believes that if we could find this crown, we could change the rats and give Khan the power to make all their lives much cleaner, better, happier, instead of living in the disgusting way that they do.

Also, Professor Badger is equally worried that if these rebel rats were looking for the crown of power that it would be complete chaos if they were to find it first.

Because with this they would take control of the Rat Kingdom even if they are not the old Kings relatives.

"So, I think we should try and find this first, but you all need to understand that many times this has been searched for over the years." He said, hoping to get agreement for this quest.

"Are we all agreed? Georgi asked, adding, "I think if anything it will be a fun day out for us all and if we take some Cherry Pie and other snacks, we can have a great time even if we find nothing. So, it's a yes then?" Using his Grandma's Cherry Pie to encourage agreement was not normally Georgi's way of putting forward an idea but he really felt that this was very important to at least try to find the crown.

"Yes, I agree. They all quickly replied. "Aussie as usual was a little worried about whether they should be doing this or not but knew that Georgi was going to do this either way.

"Maybe we should ask if we can take a Badger with us from Badger Battalion in case the rebels are there because it is too dangerous for us to go on our own! He stated, obviously worrying about the current problems.

"We will be fine Aussie, tomorrow we can discuss this, what we think happened, what could cause a City to just disappear and then we will make some plans while we are waiting for the rats to advise us of the rebels' location then we decide if they are far enough away for us to go and search. Ok?" he asked reassuringly as they all agreed completely with Georgi's suggestion.

They were just getting ready to leave when Freddie screamed," Something's coming! Incoming! Quickly! Everyone, get out of the way!" Freddie bellowed.

There was a huge white bird heading straight for them, as Freddie dived onto the floor, Alona and Georgi moved together to form a protective cover over Freddie, Aussie managed to fly out of the window to a safe distance.

Loud cracks were heard as the gigantic bird came crashing through the tree on a collision course with their tree house. "Keep down!" Aussie shouted as the unknown bird flapped as though it was out of control!

Another loud crack! As it broke more branches, followed by an even bigger crack as it came, it teetered, trying to stop itself, as it destroyed the roof of the tree house. "Oh dear" They heard, wondering if this was a bird of prey looking for its lunch. "I am terribly sorry, but I have damaged the roof of your house!" it said, ashamed of its poor flying skills. "What in bird's name are you doing, you have wrecked it!" Aussie screamed at the strange bird obviously understanding that it wasn't going to attack them! "But I don't have any idea where I am, I'm lost and of all the places I managed to land on, I destroy someone's home, this is terrible what a disaster, how can I fix this?" it asked very apologetically.

    Georgi and Alona slowly stood and helped Freddie from the floor, "It's just a treehouse Aussie, everybody is ok, just a little shocked!" Georgi stated, with Aussie still ranting at the bird. Alona looked at the two webbed feet standing on the floor of what remained of their tree house. "You are a water bird." She said and curiously asked, "How did you end up in our tree house?

"My wing is damaged, I was very hungry, had no energy and could only fly short distances with this wing like this. I realised that I could not fly any further when I saw this lake, but I didn't have the strength to fly to it. I was worried about landing on the ground and finishing up as some strange dog's dinner so I thought it would be best to rest in a tree for a short while and then continue to find something to eat. And now look at the mess I have made!" he stuttered in disbelief at its bad luck at landing on their roof.

"If you can help us fix this roof, we will help you to find some food!" Georgi offered their assistance. "It's just broken our roof and now you want to feed it, did you bang your head when it crashed onto our tree house?" Aussie asked not believing what he was hearing. "You don't even know what kind of food this bird eats, maybe it eats hedgehogs!" Aussie added sarcastically.

"What kind of bird are you, what do you eat?" Alona asked as she angrily stared at Aussie, clearly annoyed with his attitude.

"I am a Pelican, my name is Pete and I only eat fish, this was why I was going to the lake!" not amused in the slightest with Aussie's sarcasm.

"Ok, so here's what we will do, Aussie you stay here and keep Pete company and when he has the strength to go to the lake guide him to where we normally fish. Alona and Freddie grab the fishing tackle and we will go to the lake and catch Pete some fish, agreed?" Georgi knew that Aussie was far from happy with this arrangement, but he also knew from the look on Aussie's face that he was the only one who could fly down to the lake with him, so off they went to the lake.

The edge of the lake was only 5 minutes' walk from the tree house and very quickly they were catching fish and piling them on the grass behind them in readiness for when Pete arrived. "I hope Pete doesn't destroy the lake when he eventually lands here today!"

Freddie jokingly commented, to the laughter of Alona and Georgi. "I wonder where he is from, I have never seen a huge bird like this before?" Alona asked but nobody knew the answer. "We can ask him after he has eaten!" answered Georgi, "by the size of his mouth, I think he can eat quite a bit." Georgi added as the guys chuckled in agreement.

The water was very still as usual in Landon on this warm sunny day and the friends were sitting comfortably in the green grass that surrounded the lake fishing as Aussie arrived with Pete.

"Are these for me?" Pete asked excitedly, they had been fishing for about an hour, maybe a little longer as it was a very slow process. "That's plenty for me now, I don't need any more thank you very much!" Pete continued as he bent down and scooped all the remaining fish, they had caught in one gulp of his huge beak.

The pouch under his beak bulged with the fish and slowly he ate these a little each time.

"Very tasty fish you have here, really nice of you to do this for me especially after I broke the roof of your tree house!" said Pete, feeling guilty about what had happened and surprised they were now feeding him! "Yes, really very nice considering what you have done!" replied Aussie clearly, still annoyed by all this. "Aussie please stop this; Pete has already offered to help us fix the roof. Why you are being so aggressive I don't know, now stop this, this instant and let's figure out how we are going to fix this roof!" Georgi shouted annoyed at Aussie's bad manners.

"Whatever you need to carry up to the tree house I will be able to take much quicker" Pete added as he finished his fish. "I just need a little rest to allow my food to settle first" he added.

"How long do you think you will be here for," Freddie asked.

"If I can find a place to stay, I would love to be here until my wing has completely mended." He answered as Alona asked where he was from. "I'm from Pelicaland, it's a long way from here. I got separated from my group in a storm and have been unable to find them for days now. I have just been trying to find food and a place to stay" Pete told them.

"Guys, I think Pete should stay at the tree house until he has recovered, he could be like our security when we are not here, what do you think?" 'Have you completely lost your mind? There isn't enough room for him and us!" Aussie asked as he interrupted him not believing what he was hearing. Georgi totally ignored his friend and continued, "While we are fixing the roof, we can always make our place a little bit bigger" he suggested, still ignoring Aussie.

"One minute please, yesterday you suggested letting Mikey Mole join our group and now today you are asking us to allow this huge bird, who almost wrecked our treehouse, to stay with us?" Aussie stated, clearly not impressed.

"Firstly, I did not invite Mikey to join us, I suggested we set him a task and we all agreed to let him join us if he successfully achieved this goal and now, we have an injured Pelican which you don't want us to help?" Georgi replied with Alona and Freddie nodding in complete agreement with him.

"If you put it like that then ok." Aussie answered now backtracking upon seeing the others not impressed with his comments.

In reality, they were just making their tree house higher and at a later date, with additional construction, could easily make it into a second floor.

Pete started hauling things up to the tree house, where Freddie and Georgi were waiting to complete the construction.

Aussie and Alona were searching for the required materials for Pete to take to the tree house.

Alona was amused to notice that quite uncharacteristically; Aussie wasn't his normal bossy self when he was with her.

But every now and then he would disappear to check the work that Georgi and Freddie were doing, "Are you sure that it will be safe like that and that it doesn't go there before Freddie suddenly asked, "Aussie are you leaving Alona to do all the work below? Do you think this is correct?" "Just checking guys" he answered as these comments quickly sent him scurrying away because after all, he didn't want Alona to be angry with him.

Georgi and Freddie laughed at each other, "nicely done!" Said Georgi and with that they high fived each other and continued working.

After a few hours, it was finished, "I think we should all go to my Grandma's for some cherry pie because we have all done very well today." Georgi stated knowing that his offer wouldn't be refused. "Do you like Cherry Pie? He asked Pete and continued before he had a chance to answer, "My Grandma's famous in these parts for her pies."

"I must be honest, between me and you, I have never tried cherry pies or any pies for that matter" he answered, not sure what to say other than the truth.

"Ok, let's go to Grandma's, she will make you very welcome and we will have some Cha-yorchik too!"

Pete repeated "Cha-yorchik?" unsure what it was. "This is my Grandma's tea" Georgi said as Alona continued, "it's really nice,"

So, off they went Pete following Aussie and the other guys walking the short distance to Grandma's. When they arrived, Grandma was already speaking with Pete, she was very curious never having seen a Pelican before let alone sitting and speaking with one.

Georgi lovingly hugged his Grandma and asked if it would be ok for Pete to try her beautiful pie, adding that it might even help with his injured wing recovery.

"But of course," she replied, always happy to help.

Pete sampled the cherry pie and couldn't believe how good it was. "I have never eaten anything so scrumptious that didn't have any fish in it, incredible," as he ate a second piece then a third, washing it down with the green Cha-yorchik that complimented the flavour so much.

"That was absolutely delicious, I must admit the first time you mentioned tasting this I didn't think I would like it at all as there was no fish in it, but it was really good, and I hope I can visit again." Pete stated in amazement.

"Of course, you can, I'm very happy that you liked it," replied Grandma, not knowing anyone who didn't like her pies.

Grandma advised Georgi that she had a message from Mikey Mole requesting that they meet tomorrow morning, 10am at the Treehouse as he had something to show them.

"Oh good, tomorrow will be a very interesting day!" Georgi stated, looking at Grandma and adding gleefully, "maybe we will need some more cherry pie to celebrate Mikey's project tomorrow!"

"Then you best go and pick me some more cherries young man! "Many hands make light work`` She instructed the gang.

Off they went to the nearest cherry tree and picked sufficient cherries for Grandma and on returning all said goodnight. Aussie returned to the tree house to make sure that Pete arrived there ok and after bidding him goodnight also went home.

Everyone was already excited by what events would happen the next day with Mikey's project complete.

CHAPTER THREE

TESTING MOLE'S LATEST INVENTION

The following morning the sun was shining, and the sky was a beautiful light blue, everything always looked so much better in the sunshine.

But still there was something in the air, all was not correct, it was like someone was watching but there was nobody to be seen.

Most of the elders felt this, some smelled something not normal in the air but nothing unusual had been seen or reported, even though it was explained away as atmospheric, somewhere still a little apprehensive, but life in Landon continued as normal.

Georgi's gang were starting to assemble outside Georgi and his Grandma's except for Freddie who they always met on the way because he lived much closer to the tree house.

After the normal morning greeting, they set off towards the tree house.

"What do you think Mikey has created for us?" asked Aussie curiously.

"Been thinking about this all morning and haven't got a clue, now I am thinking we will have to wait just a little bit longer until he appears, not long now, 10 minutes!" he answered, giving a little chuckle.

"I also was thinking about this last night and this morning," Alona commented "and the only thing I could think of was maybe a lift system for the tree house."

"A lift system for the tree house, I think that would be disastrous." added Aussie.

"Why must you always be so negative Aussie? Every time we talk about something new you are always telling us that it will be a problem because of this or that!" Georgi asked in an annoyed tone.

"How am I negative?" Aussie enquired.

"Look at the last couple of days, we spoke about Mikey joining our gang and you were against him completing any task because it would be a catastrophe. Yesterday we spoke about Pete staying in the tree house and you were against this also!" Georgi stated clearly annoyed.

"I'm sorry if you think that is the case, but I am purely trying to ensure that all is correct." He answered.

With that Freddie appeared asking the same question they had just been discussing, "what do you think he has made?"

"We have just been saying that we are all tired of guessing and it is better to wait a few more minutes until he arrives" Georgi stated, also impatient for Mikey's arrival.

"I think it will be some kind of flying machine," added Freddie.

"A flying machine" Aussie said. "Are you…" but as he continued, he glanced at Georgi and Alona's glaring looks and changed what he was going to say, "I just hope whatever he has made works really good for us!" "Much better," added Georgi, "Much better" as he smiled at Aussie.

"Am I missing something here," asked Freddie confused, by how Aussie was speaking.

"Nah, Aussie just being more positive about things," he replied, already pleased at Aussie's response.

They arrived at the tree house and were greeted by Pete, "Good morning, guys, all is well with the tree house" he reported.

"What time is your other friend arriving here today?" He asked.

"Any time now," but as Georgi answered,

All were curious as to what to expect, as mole had said nothing about his plans, only that they were to meet him here at 10 o'clock.

Aussie was sitting on a branch eagerly awaiting moles' arrival when suddenly he heard a rumbling in the distance.

"I think the rats are coming, quickly hide!" screeched Aussie owl.

They all ran behind the tree where their den was located and waited for Aussie to tell them when the coast was clear, and they had gone.

"Hope they haven't done anything stupid with Mikey, they are always making some kind of trouble" said Georgi quietly.

Before anyone had a chance to answer, Aussie chirped, "It's ok, it's not the rats, it's Mikey. I don't believe it!" Aussie excitedly added. "Don't believe what?" asked Alona.

"You need to see this for yourself," he answered in complete disbelief.

As they appeared from behind the tree, the sound grew louder, it was a car and Mikey was driving it!

As it slowly rolled to a stop next to the tree, Mikey proudly asked, "Well, what do you think of it?"

The guys were completely stunned they had never seen anything like this before.

"How did you make this, what powers it, is it pedal powered?" excitedly asked Georgi.

GLYNN

"Most of it was actually very easy" Mikey replied, very pleased at the guy's responses.

"I took this large bottle, made a hole in the top for a roof and to get into the car, then I just added 2 poles for axles, made 4 wheels and powered it all with this large rubber band. After this it was quite straightforward to add the steering and seats for us all!"

"The roof folds back over to provide some cover if it rains and to give us some shade and because it's made from a bottle, I call it a Botmobile."

"And there you have it, do you want to go for a drive?" he asked, already knowing what the answer would be.

"Of course," they exclaimed.

They all climbed into Mikey's car with Aussie sitting on the windscreen and Pete watching from the tree house.

"Off we go!" Mikey said as they started to move forward. "Mikey this is Incredible, Amazing," commented Georgi clearly very pleased with his friend's idea.

They decided to drive all the way around Strawberry Fields.

They drove alongside the lake, waving to all the youngsters playing there and continued along the pathway surrounding the fields.

It was such a contrast of views, on the right there was the beauty of the greenery with the red of the strawberries growing while on the left was the wonderful setting of the passing trees, some fruit trees that they had visited many times to collect fruit for Grandma.

Occasionally passing some of the animal's houses that lived in Landon.

"What a great way to see Landon, never seen it like this before," said Alona, "we can see so far, so much, it's beautiful" she added.

"Mikey, this is the best thing that I have known anyone ever to make and this is for our gang?" She asked.

"Yes, this is my project, my contribution to the gang, like you asked me, so now am I a member?" he requested hoping he already knew the answer.

"I think that I can speak for everyone here when I say, Of Course!" Georgi answered with a resounding chorus of "Yeah" echoing from the others.

As they drove a further 10 minutes or so the car started to slow down.

"Is there something wrong Mikey," Alona asked as the Botmobile almost stopped.

"It just needs the rubber band twisting to charge up again, will only take 5 minutes then we will be off again, no problem" he stated proud of his creation.

While he was winding the band, he told the guys of an idea he had that would eliminate the need to do this all together.

"If we can get another rubber band the same or bigger than this one, I can connect both to the Botmobile and as one is working, it will automatically charge the second band. So, if any of you know where there is another one of these?" he said pointing to the one below their feet. "It would be so much better?" as he finished and climbed back in with the others.

"I have never seen one of those until today", Freddie answered. "Where did this one come from?" asked Georgi hoping Mikey had an answer.

"The only place I have ever seen anything like that was in Manland but it's quite a distance from here," Aussie said, thinking that they would not go because of the distance to travel.

"But we have the Botmobile!" added Georgi. "Now thanks to our latest member we can go almost anywhere, three cheers for Mikey! Hip! Hip! Hooray," shouted the gang. "Hip! Hip! Hooray," they shouted twice more.

"So, when are we going to go to Manland?" Freddie asked.

"Why not go now, we have the car so it will not take us long to go and return once we find what we want?" suggested Georgi wanting to spend some time in the car and secretly hoping to drive it at some point.

"Ok, let's go!" Freddie added, "it will be great to have even a little adventure!"

So, they started on their journey to Manland with Georgi still waiting for the right moment to speak with Mikey about driving.

"Maybe I can have a go at driving on the way back" he eagerly asked. "Yes, that will be fine," answered Mikey.

Georgi looked at his friends, their faces beaming with happiness, even Aussie was quiet since he instructed him to be more positive.

The route to Manland was very picturesque with birds singing in the trees beside them.

Very quickly they left the path that circled Strawberry Fields and were following a trail through Fruit Woods. Although it was darker with little sunlight it was still a very pleasant journey.

Occasionally they would notice other animals staring at them curious as to what this was as they went by in the Botmobile.

They drove for about 30 minutes and suddenly they were leaving the forest and out in the open again. "Are we nearly there yet", asked Freddie. "Not far now, almost there," answered Mikey.

As they turned to the right they saw a massive mountain of rubbish, almost like fields full of it. So, huge, it was bigger than Strawberry Fields.

"Where did all this come from? Alona asked. "It came from Man," Aussie answered, "we are not sure if they are storing it here or what they intend to do with it, they just pile it up and leave it or sometimes they bury it." Aussie added.

"Ok let's go" said Mikey as the car stopped, "If we can find a rubber band everything will be much better or maybe even 2 and use one for a spare." He smiled as he set off to lead the gang in their search.

There were so many different things, lots and lots of plastic bags, bottles, and cartons, so much plastic. "Ok, everyone spread out and let's get these found," Georgi instructed, realising Manland also had a horrible smell, as they trudged along looking for elastic bands.

It wasn't very long before Alona shouted that she had found a load of them, they were rolled up in some kind of ball like an ornament. Perhaps this is how they store them, she thought to herself.

"One man's trash is another man's treasure," said Mikey.

And sure enough, when the others arrived, they realised that there were about 4/5 rubber bands rolled together in a ball. "Good they will come in very handy, and we can roll it to the Botmobile.

"Wait one minute" Georgi added could we build a small boat with one of these bottles, you know in a similar fashion to how you built the Botmobile?" The others looked confused, not sure what Georgi was planning.

"Maybe, but I need time to think about it, but why a boat?" Mikey asked, also confused.

"I found this mesh material and was thinking that if we had a boat, we could use it to catch fish for Pete to eat," he said as Alona explained to Mikey about their Pelican friend.

"We would just need some way to propel it forward and something to disconnect it from the rubber band without making holes in the bottle", Mikey explained.

"The Botmobile will float but because it has holes in the bottom for the wheels it will fill up with water very quickly so it would have to be a slightly different system, but it should work.

Not sure about how you propose to catch fish better than we can using the same method as we usually do, fishing poles?" queried Mikey.

"I was thinking of dragging something like this behind us so we could take the fish but we would have this mesh so we would not scoop up the water also!" Georgi said, very pleased with his new idea.

"We will take the mesh with us then," said Freddie and at least we can use it for something else if we don't need it", he suggested.

"Is there anything else that we need while we are here or are we all finished? Alona asked, "We should have brought a picnic and we could have stopped somewhere nice on the way back.

"We could if only we knew we were going out in a newly invented Botmobile!" Laughed Aussie but also thinking it would have been a good idea.

After everything was safely loaded Georgi took the driver's seat and they set off for the return journey under Mikey's instructions.

Georgi found it very easy to drive only having to steer whilst watching for any possible obstacles he was clearly enjoying himself.

"Can we go and show my Grandma our new Botmobile Mikey?", Georgi asked as they started the return journey, "I think we should have a small celebration for our new member and his wonderful Botmobile!"

"A wonderful idea" Aussie said, thinking about Cherry Pie.

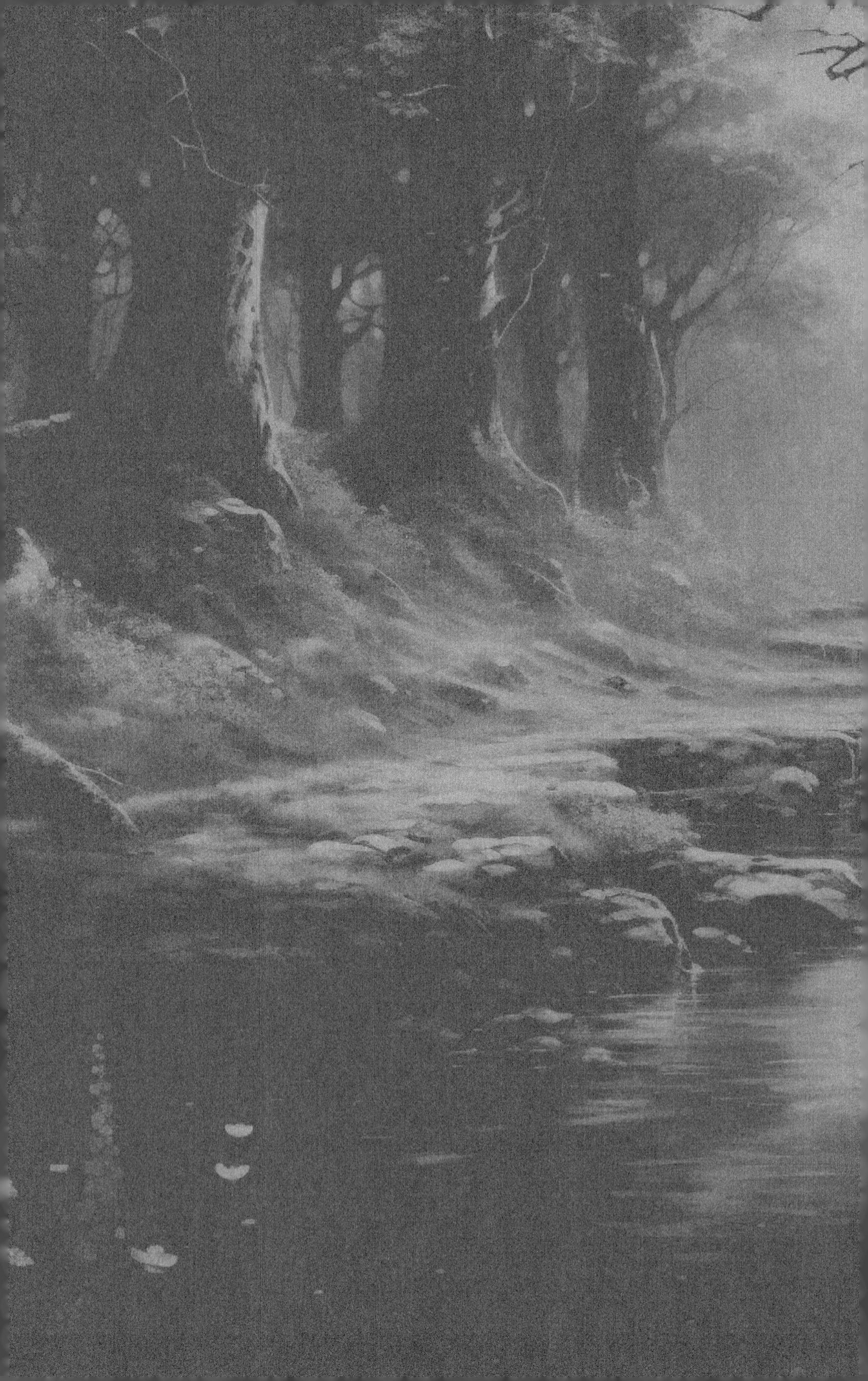

CHAPTER FOUR

IT'S A RAT RACE

As they arrived back in Landon they felt like celebrities, almost everyone living next to Strawberry Fields rushed to line the dirt path to see this new contraption, youngsters with parents, Grandparents all looked on in amazement as they had never seen anything even remotely like this Botmobile.

Upon reaching Georgi's Grandma's she also was waiting and as they stopped beside her, she said," My word, I have never seen anything like this before, where did it come from?" "We have Mikey Mole to thank for this as it is his creation. Grandma, you need to go for a ride in this, one day very soon, it's absolutely incredible, Landon looks so much bigger, more beautiful from the Botmobile!"

he said to his clearly impressed Grandmother with Mikey blushing with pride.

Other people started to look at this unusual machine, a plastic bottle on wheels that carried people and they all asked many questions.

They sat and enjoyed Cherry Pie and Cha-yorchik and were so proud of their friend Mikey and his achievements as he proudly answered questions about his new machine.

Their next outing in the car was a return to Manland.

"So, guys I have an idea how we can change the Botmobile a little to use it as a fishing boat! First, we fix two paddle wheels, one on each side to power it through the water.

Then we need something to steer it with but each of these things needs to be attached higher than the water or we will just sink if too much water gets inside." With this he showed the guys some drawings that he had done with the adaptations he was proposing.

"These two circular paddles are fixed to the sides; I can connect these to the Botmobile's main power, or we can work these by hand. They are fixed at the centre, which will not be in the water and if we have any steering controls on the outside again, we will not have any water problems with this. And although I have some things, I can use to complete this, we do need some other parts from Manland to finish it off. So, what do you think?" he asked, feeling proud of himself especially when something creative was being realised.

"These circular paddles turn, which is what moves us across the water? And this piece of plastic will steer us in the direction which we want to go?" Freddie asked.

"Exactly"

"And what happens when all the water starts to enter where the wheels are? Aussie questioned.

"This is why we can only use this for a small, limited time but I am sure it will be more than long enough to drag the net behind us as we return back to land. The holes around the wheels are small and I plan to reduce these to make them even smaller. We just need to go onto the lake as quickly as possible, deploy the net and make our way back with the fish in the net!"

"To make sure it is perfectly safe it will be easy to test this by driving onto the water and we will see how much water actually leaks into the Botmobile," said Mikey continuing to answer Aussie's question. "A very good Safety precaution" commented Alona.

"And I think, if necessary, Pete can help tow us out if we have any problems so for me the worst-case scenario is we might get a little wet!" Georgi added as they all laughed at the idea of splashing about in the water.

"Afterall, necessity is the mother of invention, said Alona, pleased.

They all headed off in the Botmobile to the lake as Pete and Aussie flew on ahead. Pete was also hoping for a good paddle in the clear blue water.

Upon arrival Aussie asked Pete if he could check the water levels around the edge of the lake so that they could find the best place to roll the Botmobile in the water for their test.

Too deep would be too dangerous and maybe difficult to get the Botmobile out again so shallow water was what they needed.

As the guys arrived Pete had found a good place to test and was merrily paddling in the water singing about all the tasty fish for him.

"Come on in guys, the water is lovely" he shouted as they approached.

"First we need to get this test out of the way, then we can enjoy ourselves!" also wanting to relax in the water.

The guys climbed into the Botmobile and as they sat there waiting Pete picked up the Botmobile in his beak with ease and placed it in the water and waited for instructions to adjust its position.

"All is good so far!" stated Mikey as they checked that all the wheels were submerged.

Alona was keeping a record of the time in the water and Mikey was now checking the amount of water that was seeping inside.

"I think we could use this for much longer than I initially believed because there is much less water coming in than I originally expected." Mikey commented very pleased with his observations.

"Is there any way that we could capture this water and just channel it back to the lake out of here?" Georgi asked, not wanting any water at all.

"Think this will be as good as it gets. But don't worry I can put a small drain in the bottom with a plug so it will be easy to remove any water quickly" he answered.

"Maybe Pete can pull us out into the lake, and we can catch some fish while we are here, we have the net?" suggested Freddie "Ooo, Yes please!" Pete quickly answered.

"Ok but not too far out we don't want to sink to the bottom!" added Georgi with a smile.

Pete quickly moved to the front of the Botmobile and started to push the guys slowly out into the lake.

"Everything ok?" he asked as he gently pushed them a little further.

"Wonderful Pete, much better than I expected," said a very pleased mole.

"Right then guys time to get this net in the water and catch some fish!" Aussie stated, seeing they were already quite far out.

The net they had made from the materials acquired at Manland was a simple design, it simply looped over the Botmobile's roof and was held in place by sliding it down, so it rested behind Alona and Freddie.

Once the net was in the water Pete simply took hold of the Botmobile's front in his beak and paddled backwards while trying to continue his song about all these wonderful fish for me!

As his mouth was already busy with the towing the words were not very clear but with all the guys laughing everyone understood what he was singing about.

Mikey kept a check on the water levels, Freddie and Alona were watching the net and could see the cable slowly cutting into the plastic behind their seats, but this was just the weight of the net and its contents.

"Once you leave the water Pete, please don't stop because I do not know if the Botmobile can pull all this extra weight and I do not want all your fish to swim away if we stop."

"Then I will definitely keep going, don't worry about that!" Pete mumbled, still pulling it with his beak.

Mikey started his creation and although slower than Pete, it was able to haul the net from the water. "So, everything is ok with you pulling it out? Pete asked but he was already rushing to see what was in the net for his dinner.

When the net started to appear, Pete got even more and more excited and as it spilled onto the ground at the edge of the lake, he quickly noticed that there was not just fish in the net but also a large turtle!

Who was not very happy in the slightest, "What is the meaning of this?" he snapped as he gulped down a fish beside him.

"My fish, what are you doing?" screamed Pete as he grabbed a few fish for himself.

"What am I doing, I was enjoying a nice relaxing swim, then I was pulled into this net of yours and you ask, what I am doing! Now, you begrudge me a few fish! He answered, clearly angry at his demise.

"Apologies but you are welcome to join me and share these fish if you want?"

"Maybe, some other time, I need to go now." And with that he turned, walked into the lake.

"Ok, another time, bye for now" Pete responded quickly as just the turtle's head was now visible.

"Bye and thanks for the fish." He replied as his head disappeared under the water and he was gone.

Pete continued to feast on the remaining fish from the net as Mikey and the others surveyed the Botmobile.

"You see all that time we were on the lake and there is still only a small amount of water that has leaked in." Mikey commented as Freddie pointed out, "And one large angry turtle!" he said with a chuckle with the others joining his laughter.

"If I make a small hole here then plug it with a correctly fitting branch then when we are finished, we will just remove the branch until the water drains out. With the net cutting into the back, we just need a piece of wood between the cable and the plastic which will stop any further problems with this." Mikey was feeling really pleased with himself as Georgi asked, "Where's Alona?"

"She went to take some strawberries for us so we can all eat together but I think Pete will be finished very quickly indeed!" Freddie replied as Pete apologised and agreed to wait until Alona returned.

"I'm here!" Alona added walking towards them with a couple of really nice-looking strawberries.

So, they all sat down and ate with the main subject being how wonderful Mikey's adaptations and inventions were.

The strawberries were nice and sweet, and Pete's fish were really tasty too.

Mikey told the guys about his latest invention, a Botmobile, which could go underwater, like a fish below the surface of the lake.

"Now for me that is special, I have never been underwater, and I am not sure if it is possible, would it really work, how can we breathe underwater? Said Aussie thrilled at his idea but doubtful that it would work.

"We just hold our breath!" Freddie answered. "Been doing it all my life!" Everyone laughed except Aussie who was still trying to understand how it could be possible.

"It would be very spectacular to see life under the water in the Lake and I am sure if anyone can do this, you can Mikey after all look what he has already achieved!" added Alona excited at the prospect of seeing a brave new world beneath the water.

"Birds don't like water and how we will know if it works, how's it possible to test something like that safely?" commented Aussie now believing it wouldn't be safe enough.

"Firstly as long as we do not go in water that is too deep we should be ok to test it, secondly if Freddie can be in the water beside us he could communicate with others on the surface, obviously to test it only those that are needed would be onboard, thirdly if there is a problem we signal to Freddie and he instructs you guys above to use the Botmobile to pull it out maybe Pete can be on standby for this also if his help is needed. And there you have it, simple, safe testing of Mikey's new invention. What are you going to call it?" Georgi asked, satisfied that he had answered the question fully.

"A BotMarine " stated Mikey. "It's a bottle designed for the marine of the lake, but I still have work to do on this project, it's a little bit tricky because it needs to be completely waterproof, no water can be allowed to get in at all. But now I need to adapt the Botmobile for fishing! So, that and other projects will need to wait" he said excited about his current project.

"Mikey you are Amazing!" Georgi said.

"You're the bee's knees Mikey!" Alona added as the others cheered.

After eating they quickly cleared away the net and headed to Manland to collect the other parts that Mikey needed to make the Botmobile into a boat.

Pete went to the tree house to rest after his wonderful but quite large meal.

During the trip to Manland the conversation was only about the adventures they could have on a boat, but their adventures hadn't even started in their latest form of transport.

Driving through the wonderful countryside on a beautiful day was something that they all loved. Upon reaching Manland the guys split up into groups to find the necessary things for Mikey to make a wonderful boat.

Alona had suggested using some plastic bottles to use as the fins for the paddles, but Mikey had seen some small fans when he had been here before and hoped they would still be there as he thought these would have been ideal for what he had in mind.

But whatever they used the guys now knew they would soon have a fabulous machine that could go on land or on water.

When they had everything that they wanted Mikey was still searching he had another idea and found some parts that they did not take with them but hid them for the next time that they came.

They left with the necessary parts. Anything that they couldn't take was hidden with the other stuff that they found.

They drove only a short way from Manland only to find that their path had been blocked by a group of rats who had seen them go this way and were waiting for them to return.

They had created a barricade made of tree branches, bracken, and twigs. In front of this was parked their machine which they called a Rat Peddler.

"Leave and fetch Professor Badger, tell him something is happening here" he whispered as quietly as possible, so they did not overhear.

Aussie just flew off and as he left them, he said to Georgi, "be careful I don't trust these dirty animals!" "Neither do I!" he answered, not knowing if he had heard him as he quickly flew off on his mission.

The rat's car was a very thin paper box with wheels which was powered by a large number of pedals and propelled by a large number of rats. As expected, it wasn't clean at all, maybe it had never been clean. The wheels were made from quite small bottle tops but although these were all the same size they didn't match.

"Nice machine! But is it as quick as ours?" he asked pointing to their car as the other rats with him sniggered.

There were maybe fifteen to twenty rats in total, so they were well outnumbered standing on two legs with tails that were bigger than the rats' bodies.

GEORGI AND FRIENDS

"Not sure," replied Georgi wondering what was going on and why these animals were so dirty, why didn't they wash he thought.

"We have never raced anyone before, so is yours fast?" he asked curiously looking at the rat's pedal powered machine.

Mikey advised Georgi that with the small size of the wheels compared to theirs it couldn't possibly go any faster than the Botmobile.

"However fast they pedalled because of the small wheels it would be very nippy but nowhere near as fast as theirs." He whispered to Georgi.

"Good to know that Mikey" he said with a wink in his direction.

"So, are you from Rat City?"

"No, we don't live in Rat City, they have far too many stupid rules and a crazy King!" he answered as the others burst into loud laughter.

Georgi pretended to laugh along with these rats while discreetly beckoning Aussie to him.

"Now we need to find out who are the better designers and builders, of this type of machines, folk from Landon or us Rats!"

"Not sure if we have time for a race today." A worried Georgi replied, looking at a very worried Alona.

All of the rats then closed ranks surrounding Georgi, Alona, Freddie, and Mikey around the car as they bared their long teeth.

Gradually the rats moved closer and closer to the gang and manoeuvred themselves between the gang and the car.

"We are going to race for each other's cars!" The Rat leader declared.

"No! We just finished our car today and we are not racing anyone yet!" answered Mikey as Georgi moved Alona behind him to protect her.

"You are not in a position to refuse! We insist! If we win, we will take your car, if you win you take our car, but this won't happen! He declared as the guys looked anxiously at Georgi, unsure what to do.

"Or we cannot race, declare us the winners and take your car anyway!" He added as all the rebels agreed and laughed loudly.

"Ok, so where are you proposing that we race?" Georgi asked quite calmly considering the situation they were in.

"We will start from here, to the end of the path, first one there is the winner! Your white hedgehog friend will stay here and start the race, and if there is any funny business like you deciding you want to run for it, we will return for her, do you understand?" he instructed, pointing to Alona.

"Agree! Georgi replied worriedly wondering what would become of them but all the time trying to slow things down, to give Aussie a chance to return with Professor badger before something serious occurred.

"How far is this course we are competing on?" trying to waste some time.

"It's not very long, not for us anyway!" he said bragging how fast their car was as many of the rats rushed around to clear the blocked path so that the race could begin.

"So, get into your car and get ready, your white hedgehog friend needs to stand there with this leaf held in the air and countdown from 3, when she reaches zero, she needs to quickly lower the leaf and the race starts, understand?" making sure his commands were fully understood.

"It's a Rat Race!" he added to squeals of laughter from the other rats.

"I'll explain it to Alona as she sometimes doesn't understand everything," signalling to Alona not to speak as he knew that she was about to say that she understood, and he had some important instructions for her also.

"Georgi quickly said to Alona, "Whatever happens you go straight home when we race, understand?" "Yes, I understand," answered Alona. "As soon as we start!" Georgi commanded, emphasizing the importance of his order.

Georgi climbed into the Botmobile as Alona, who was clearly shaking, took the leaf and was guided where to stand for the start of the race.

"Ok," said the rebels as Alona raised the leaf in the air.

"So, what are the rules?" Georgi asked, trying to delay things a little longer.

"There are no rules!" their leader quickly answered as he pushed for the race to start.

"And if we have a breakdown?" he continued.

"Then you lose!" Followed by even more laughter, from all the rats.

"So, enough talk, let's race!!" He declared to cheers of "Yeah!" from his followers.

"Is everything ready Mikey" Georgi asked. "We are ready to go!" "Do you have a plan?" asked Freddie hopefully. "I hope so, I hope so!" he replied as Alona shouted, "Three!" The rats started laughing at them clearly believing they were going to easily win.

"Two! The rebels' laughter intensified. "One!" but with this the rats had already set off early, laughing hysterically.

"Go Mikey", Georgi shouted, followed by "Run to home Alona" as they hurtled past her. Mikey looked in front of them seeing them already moving closer to the rats and then looked behind to see Alona running towards home.

He didn't really have a plan, but he knew Alona would meet up with Professor Badger somewhere between there and home, but it was probably too late to help them.

"Should have known those rats would cheat and go on one instead of zero!" Freddie stated, "So, what are we going to do?" he asked.

"Professor Badger should be on his way by now, we just need to play for time until he gets here!" Georgi informed them but hoping to come up with another plan.

"It's ok," Mikey screamed, "we are catching up with them very quickly now, no problems!" he said with a broad smile.

"But that's the problem!" Georgi replied. "They are not going to let us take their car nor are they going to let us keep ours if they win! Somehow, we need to stall for time until help arrives! But how can we do that?" "We have almost caught up with them!" Mikey interrupted.

Now alongside the rebels' car they went over a hill, it looked like the rest of the way was downhill. "Do they have a weight advantage now that it is downhill and there are many of them?" Georgi asked, with Mikey starting to get a little worried.

But before Mikey could answer they were quickly coming alongside the rats' car!

Which was now trying to attack them as they approached.

As they passed, they were suddenly being attacked by a large number of long, rat tails that were whipping them.

Mikey was on the other side of the car driving and was far enough away to avoid them.

Georgi stood and turned his back, so it was facing the rats and at the same time instructed Freddie to get down on the floor of the car to avoid them.

After they hit the spikes on Georgi's back, they soon stopped.

Strangely as they moved further and further in front of the rebels, they could only hear the rats howling with laughter, something was very wrong!

As he looked back at the rat's car the loud howling laughter could still be heard but then the rats turned left off the path and disappeared out of sight!

Georgi could only think that for some unknown reason they were going back for Alona!

"Stop the car Mikey", Georgi screamed, "Quickly! Turn around and go back!" he ordered.

"I can't, they have done something to the brakes!! And I cannot move the steering" shouted Mikey, "I have disengaged the power, but we will not start to slow down until this hill levels!", as he tried to stay calm and not to panic.

"Georgi, you drive, and I will see if I can fix it!" They changed places and Mikey then disappeared under the seats to try to fix the car.

He shouted up to the guys, "Those evil rats have cut through the line connecting our brakes in two places and the part is missing from the steering!"

"Can you fix it?" Georgi asked eager to return and find Alona.

"Unfortunately, not," Mikey said, as he again re-appeared.

With that Aussie appeared having returned from contacting Professor Badger, "Stop the car! Stop the car!" he shouted.

"We can't the rats have sabotaged the brakes!" replied Mikey.

"You must, there is a cliff ahead!!"

Now Georgi realised why the rebels were laughing, they didn't want to steal the car, they wanted to destroy it and the gang along with it!

"Freddie, can you use your tongue to help us stop?"

With that Freddie fired his tongue at an approaching plant. It stretched and stretched but there was no difference in their speed, they weren't slowing at all.

Very quickly Freddie had to give up or risk irreparable damage to his tongue.

"Do something quickly, you are almost at the cliff" Aussie was now screaming at the guys.

"So, there is only one thing left to do! We must save ourselves; we must jump!" Said Georgi.

Freddie quickly leapt to safety while Georgi wrapped himself around Mikey, aware that he had little in the way of protection.

Mikey glanced and could see the cliff edge fast approaching, "Quickly Georgi! Quickly!"

"Just get ready to hit the floor! Because I am rolled up in a ball, I will need to release you soon or we will just roll down the hill." He explained.

With the edge of the cliff getting closer and closer they rolled off the back of the Botmobile.

They resembled a wheel with Mikey in the centre, his feet sticking out at one end and his head at the other.

As they hit the ground Georgi's spikes cushioned the impact while they bounced a few times uphill.

Georgi realised that they would soon start rolling downhill and instructed Mikey to get ready to land on the ground.

Mikey just had time to acknowledge when he was flung by Georgi and quickly felt the hard ground below him as he rolled and rolled across the path.

"Are you guys ok," Aussie asked clearly worried about his friends.

"I'm ok, what about Freddie? Georgi asked while walking towards Mikey.

"He's coming now, boy that was close, another few seconds and you would have been over the edge of that cliff!" They both moved towards Mikey who was now lying motionless on the ground.

"Mikey! Mikey! Please be ok Mikey!" Georgi said as he lifted his friend's lifeless head.

"Please be ok" his voice croaking he added, "this is all, my fault, my stupid idea for Mikey to make something for us and this is how we end up!"

"How can something like this happen and be your fault if you don't know it is going to happen?" asked Aussie.

"You guys, ok?" Freddie said as he approached them.

"It's Mikey, he won't come round!" Georgi answered clearly worried.

The guys feared the worst with Mikey laying there completely motionless, Georgi had never lost anyone before.

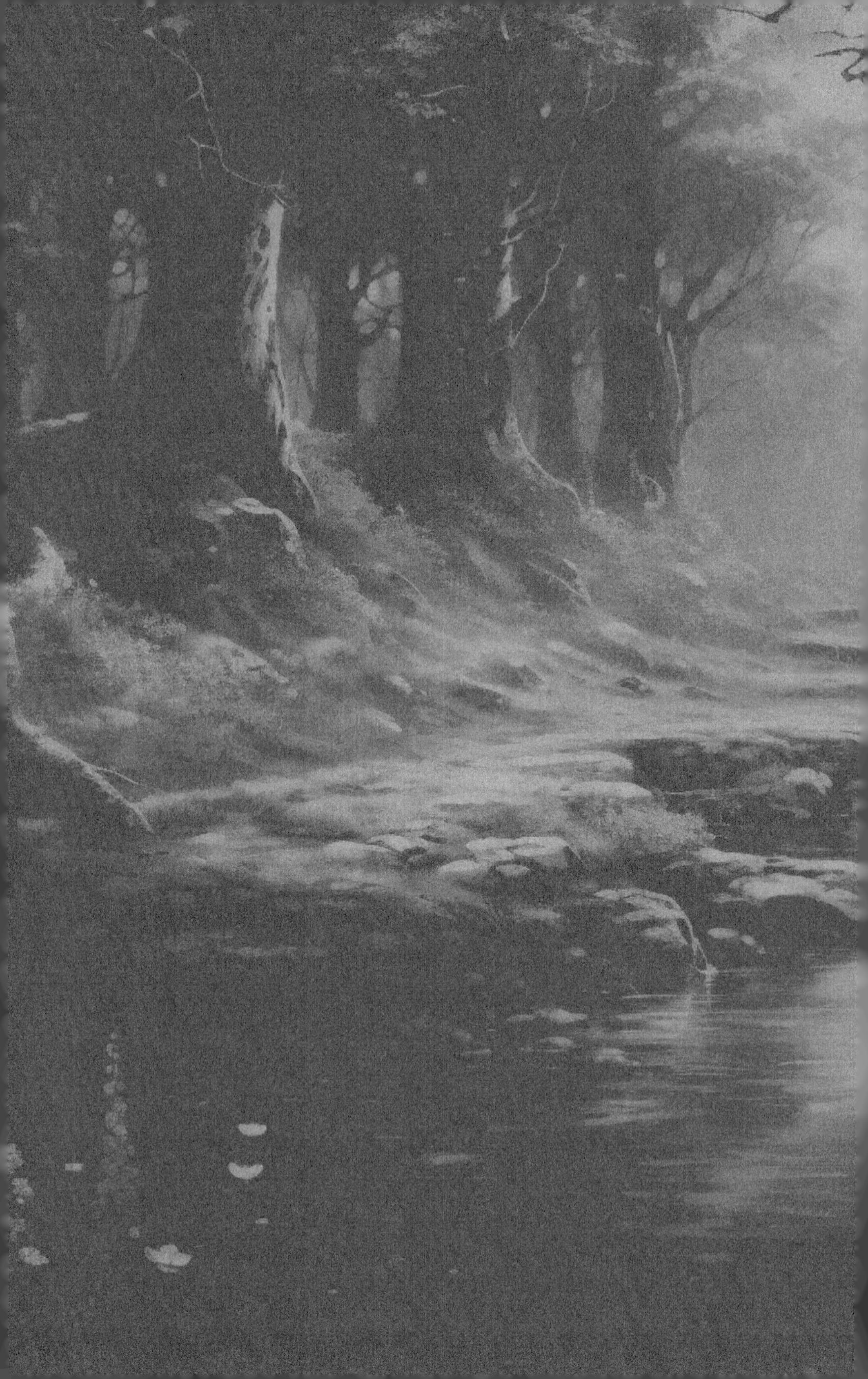

CHAPTER FIVE

FEEDING PETE, THE PELICAN

"Is he breathing?" Aussie asked.

"Check around his mouth and nose for signs of breathing." Freddie suggested.

"Nothing, right what can we do now?" Georgi asked anxiously.

"Let's take him home, Professor Badger should meet us on the way, maybe he knows what to do?" Aussie suggested, knowing that the Professor should be here any minute now, "he'll know what to do".

"Ok" answered Georgi, picking up Mikey's limp body into his arms and started walking.

His thoughts went to the happier times they spent together with Mikey only wanting to be their friend and now this.

Tears welled up in his and his friends' eyes and as they started walking up the hill to return a tear fell on Mikey's cheek.

Georgi brushed it away and continued walking.

All of a sudden, there was a sneeze and a chorus of "Bless You!" from all of them.

"Mikey, was that you? Georgi asked, his eyes filling up with even more tears.

"What happened? Where am I? Why are you carrying me? Oh, I remember! My Botmobile!" Mikey Mole shouted.

You're Ok! You're Ok!" Georgi blurted out joyfully, unable to hide his happiness. "We thought that we had lost you and feared the worst." He added gleefully as he sat him down in the grass next to them.

"You're Ok! This is so wonderful! How are you feeling?" he asked as the guys gathered around him.

"I'm ok, just a slight headache. Think I bumped my head when I landed" he answered wondering what all the fuss was about.

When Mikey felt well enough to move the guys helped him up and continued walking up the hill that not long ago, they were hurtling down.

As they neared the top, they couldn't believe their eyes. Something very familiar was waiting at the top of the hill.

"Are my eyes playing tricks on me or do you guys see what I see?" Freddie asked, unable to understand what was really in front of them.

The guy's pace quickened, Georgi added, "I see it, but I don't believe it! Is this possible?"

"I really hope so!" said Mikey, now almost running towards the top of the hill.

There in front of them stood the Botmobile! It was completely intact, not broken and smashed like they would have expected it to be the next time that they saw it.

"How is this possible?" Freddie asked what everyone was thinking.

"Maybe you managed to turn it around somehow?" Thought Aussie.

"Even if we had managed to turn it around, I disconnected the power to the driver, so it would never have made it this far up the hill. Plus, how did it go past us without us seeing it?" asked Mikey not really caring about the answers as he was just happy that it was standing there in front of him.

"You were well out of it and wouldn't have seen it anyway Mikey!" Freddie answered as everyone including Mikey laughed.

At that moment a familiar voice was heard saying "There you are! I have been looking for you guys everywhere! Thought I was too late. When I caught the Botmobile as it went over the edge, I brought it up here but then realised that you guys were not inside. I could only see the car in the dust cloud that it had made. So, I went back to look for you, was starting to think you had fallen out until I saw some movement up here!" Pete explained, pleased that they were all ok.

"But how did you know where we were in the first place?" asked Georgi.

"When Aussie was on his way to the Professor, he asked me to go to you thinking that I could scoop you all away or something to save you from the rats and then I came here, and he went to the Professor." Pete informed them.

"Thank you so much Pete! You are the greatest! You're a Gem! I thought that my best, ever creation had been destroyed and was laying in pieces at the bottom of that cliff!" said Mikey feeling so much better now.

"Aussie, can you and Pete find Alona then one of you stay with her until we arrive the other can return and tell us where to meet up?" Georgi asked, still worried about her. "Before you go, where is Professor Badger?"

"He should be on his way here but it's a much longer route on the paths. It will be much better if you wait here until he arrives. At least then we won't have to worry about you as well! Think we have had enough worrying for today" he said, happy that all agreed with him for once and hoping that nothing else was going to happen on this day.

Pete and Aussie set off to find Alona, Mikey waited by his beloved Botmobile while Georgi and Freddie collected some vines and a piece of bark so that Mikey could fix the brakes and steering.

A few minutes later Professor Badger arrived.

Georgi and the guys explained what had happened as the Professor checked Mikey's injuries.

"Just a few lumps and bumps young mole, a good rest and you will be as good as new!" he declared, pleased that everyone was now ok!

"So, let's go back to Landon so your families know you are all safe and well." The Professor added.

"First we need to find Alona, I sent her back on her own, worried that something would happen to her" The Professor put Georgi's mind at rest.

"I met and spoke with her on the way here, she's ok, heading back to Landon and I know she will be pleased to see all of you, so let's make tracks." He said with a smile.

As they started to return Mikey asked if they could take it slowly to which Freddie replied, "I agree, I think we have had more than enough fast adventures today!" This even made the Professor chuckle.

After travelling for about fifteen to twenty minutes they met Aussie returning and could see Pete ahead walking with Alona. It was such a relief to Georgi and the guys that all the gang was back together again plus everyone was safe and well, including the Botmobile.

When they caught up with Alona, Georgi had earlier cut the power to the wheels so they could easily coast up to them. Alona's happiness was obvious to see as she ran towards the car. "I'm so happy that you are all ok" she shouted gleefully.

But I still need to do something about these rebel rats!" added Professor Badger.

"I think we need a plan to catch them because life will not go back to being normal with those rodents running free!" he said obviously in deep thought.

"Let's get you guys safely home then I need to summon an emergency council meeting so that we can decide what to do about these varmints!" and with this they all set off for Landon once again.

Upon reaching Landon Georgi invited the guys for Cherry Pie and Cha-yorchik but all wanted to rest at home so they agreed to meet the next day to help Mikey make the conversions to the Botmobile so it could be used for fishing on the lake.

Aussie was much happier as it was in Landon which was a much safer option.

Early the next day the guys and Alona all met at Mikey's workshop.

Mikey had already made the paddle wheels; they assembled the rear paddle which would be used to steer it when it was on the water and began fixing the modified parts to the Botmobile.

"Ok, let's collect Pete and take it to the lake to catch some fish! Proclaimed Georgi.

Mikey drove it out of the workshop then they proceeded towards the lake stopping at the tree house for Pete.

"It's amazing" commented Pete upon seeing Mikey's adaptations to the Botmobile.

"You make some really incredible things Mikey!" he said as Mikey blushed.

Making their way to the lake Aussie and Pete flew alongside in the cool afternoon breeze.

To reduce the amount of time that the Botmobile would actually be in the water, Freddie had a great idea using Pete to tow them out to the middle of the lake which would allow them to power it back to the shore with the fish. And if needed Pete could also tow them back because they were unsure as to how the weight of the fish would affect the operation of the Botmobile and did not even know if they had enough power to pull the extra weight.

As they arrived at their destination, they secured the net to the rear of the vehicle to which Pete then flew down, grabbing the net in his feet and began towing them into the middle of the lake where they believed the fish were.

For the guys it was a new but wonderful sensation as they cut through the still clear water of the beautiful lake. Looking at the lake from a position on the water was breathtaking with the green of strawberry fields and the majestic trees standing tall in the background like soldiers watching over them. Floating on the water was not new to Freddie being a frog, but even he enjoyed looking through the clear bottom and frequently seeing the wildlife that lived in the lake without having to get wet.

"It's so quiet, such a wonderful but different view of Landon, we should make a picnic one day and come out here to relax in the boat, it would be wonderful! She happily sighed as the water occasionally splashed them, but this just added to the enjoyable moment.

Everything was so calm and quiet only the sound of the water as the Botmobile powered its way through the water.

Freddie signalled to Pete that this was far enough upon which he released the net and let it splash into the water.

As they waited for the net to fully submerge in the water Georgi had an idea based on what Alona had previously said, "as it is so pleasant here, I think we should make a picnic today after we catch these fish and spend some time here on the water,"

"Great idea and I can take a swim," said Freddie, already feeling the need to just jump into the water.

The net slowly disappearing beneath the surface of the water was the signal for Mikey to start the Botmobile moving.

Mikey put the new paddle assemblies into motion. "All is good so far, but we are going in the wrong direction.

"Oh no! It's connected the wrong way round!" Mikey said, looking down at the paddle wheels.

"Ok, no need to panic! What can we do to correct this?" Asked Aussie, worried about what they could do to fix this.

"Firstly, disconnect the power to stop us moving too far in the wrong direction!" Georgi calmly answered.

"We can always get Pete to tow us back!" he continued.

"Can you attach the net to the front and go backwards to the land?" asked Aussie.

"Great idea!" Georgi said, confident that it was not a major problem. "Will you be able to correct this Mikey and how is the water level inside? He said, referring to the water that was leaking in.

"It would take too long to change the paddle assemblies to correct this, but the water is at an acceptable level so at the minute it is not a problem. I agree with Aussie that the best course of action is to move the nets to the front and reverse it back to land! Mikey added.

The guys agreed and Mikey slowly started to turn it around as he did so the guys removed the net from the rear and secured it to the front.

Aussie checked everything when it was complete, and Mikey started the paddles and it moved slowly backwards towards the land as the paddle wheels splashed their way through the water.

Slowly gathering speed, they were finally moving in the direction they wanted.

Pete was relieved that all was now ok as he was very tired after towing them out there originally and then he headed back to land for a much-needed rest.

Then they felt a sudden tug as the Botmobile began hauling the net, the extra weight straining as they were suddenly jolted.

About halfway back Alona asked, "is it me or are we slowing down?" "Yes, I believe you are right! We are definitely slowing but why? Is something wrong Mikey? Georgi said, unsure what was happening.

"No nothing is wrong, everything is working. It must be the weight of the net and the fish dragging us and causing us to slow down." Mikey answered while he continued to check the Botmobile.

"I will go and take a look," said Aussie as he flew off in the direction of the net.

Thankfully they were still moving when Aussie returned and informed the guys that the net was completely full and he was very happy to report that it was without turtles, referring to the previous episode when they caught Andre the turtle.

"Guys, do you know that you are sitting much deeper in the water than you were a few minutes ago?" he said, already seeing the alarm on the others' faces.

With the extra weight at the nose end where the net was now connected, it was being pulled underwater.

Mikey appeared from below and exclaimed "Guys we have a big problem with the water! Because the weight of the fish is pulling that part of the Botmobile underwater, it is forcing water inside at a far greater rate than before! We will sink very quickly if we do not act now!"

"Aussie quickly fetched Pete, maybe he can help somehow!" Georgi said, the water reaching his ankles, but Aussie was already on his way.

"I think I could make a hole in the net to release some of the fish!" said Freddie offering his idea.

"Too dangerous you could easily get tangled up in the netting then we would have another problem!" Mikey answered. "Then I could jump in the water and push! You would have less weight here plus a little more power." He said, not sure what else to suggest.

"Nice idea but again I think it would be too dangerous for you to help to push us" answered Georgi.

"Although you not being on board would help us stay afloat longer it would only be a matter of seconds." Mikey added, "We need something else!" looking down and seeing the water now up to his knees.

"Would it help if Pete's weight was on the other end to balance us?" Alona asked, unsure what else they could do.

By now the guys were sitting on the edge of the Botmobile trying to keep their feet out of the water.

As Alona made this comment a voice came from the water, beside them, "thankfully you haven't caught me this time!" followed by a loud chuckle. "Are you sinking? He asked, "Can I be of any assistance?"

Mikey explained the problem and Andre Turtle believed he had an answer.

"If I go underneath your craft and lift you from the water will this help drain the water?"

"Yes, if you can do this it should give us time to drain the water out!" Mikey answered.

"Thank you so much for doing this, because I was starting to think that we were history!" Mikey said with a smile.

With that Mikey disconnected the power, it slowed very quickly and as it stopped Mikey asked if he could push them back enough to stop them being dragged deeper under the water.

"Yes of course!" Andre answered as he disappeared under the water.

They slowly started moving backwards and when it was almost level the guys looked through the bottom as Andre's green shell appeared and started to lift them from the water.

"Freddie, as you are the best swimmer, can you go down and remove the three plugs that I installed, it will drain the water out much quicker?" asked Mikey while Freddie looked at the others and realised there was only himself that should do this job.

"Ok!" he said, removing his red tunic, handing it to Alona to keep dry as Mikey pointed to the location of the three plugs that he must remove.

Freddie waded towards the plugs and then dived under the water to remove them.

Loud rushes of water could be heard from underneath as Freddie removed the plugs as Aussie returned very curious as to what was happening.

"What's going on, it looks like you are floating above the water?" quickly followed by "where is Freddie?" Aussie asked worried that things were now much worse.

As they explained to Aussie what had occurred and why they were apparently floating above the water and that they were on a turtle, Freddie reappeared having removed the three plugs to drain the water.

Before anyone knew he was there, Freddie spat a stream of water at Aussie hitting him on the face and almost causing him to lose his balance!

"What was that? Oh, there you are! Why are you spitting water at me, with the pressure of the water you could have knocked me over the edge, you foolish frog!" Aussie snapped while the others laughed for the first time in what seemed like ages as Aussie felt relief seeing them all happy.

"Where is Pete?" Alona asked. "He is coming, did not have the energy after towing you out here to fly all the way, so he landed in the water and is making his way here as fast as he can." Aussie answered, speaking quite loudly to be heard over the noise of the water emptying from the Botmobile.

The sound of the water was almost like they were stuck on a rock at the edge of a large waterfall and with the thunder of the water as it crashed against Andre's shell.

"Not much more water left now." Mikey shouted to keep Andre up to date with what was happening.

Upon saying this, Pete arrived almost out of breath as he rushed to his friends.

"So, have you guys got a plan of action after all the water is drained?" shouted Andre.

"The problem that we have is that the net is too big and unlike last time that we fished it is too full!" Exclaimed Mikey "hopefully most of the fish have swum away by now so it should be much easier to pull now." With this Freddie said that he would take a quick look at the net as he was wet already.

"Try only to go as close as you need to, ok?" asked Georgi not wanting any other problems as Freddie nodded and dived into the lake.

Mikey continued, "Once the water is out, I think with the help of Pete and Andre we can return to land. The only other alternative is to empty the nets first and make them smaller for next time. If Andre can help to push us along while Pete can push from the side and hold the other end down to keep us as level as possible, I'm sure that we will be fine." Mikey concluded.

"I understand that without the fish we would have no problem returning but this is what we came out here for anyway. So, I believe we can easily do this with a little help from Pete and Andre." Said Georgi now confident that with the added assistance, that there would not be any more problems.

"After all the fish is for me and of course I will help plus even in the worst-case scenario you can always jump on my back so I will guarantee you will get back to land in one piece, maybe a little wet but definitely in one piece." He commented with a half-smile as his stomach started rumbling indicating his hunger.

Everybody started giggling with the sound of his tummy and Alona added, "we must at least try to return with the fish for the sake of Pete's tummy!" she said as everyone laughed.

Just then Freddie returned and reported that their assumption was correct. "Wow! When you see the size of that net underwater it is definitely two or three times bigger than we need. But now it is not being pulled along most of the fish have swum away. But we will scoop up more fish as the net moves in the water. There was a huge school of fish when I first saw it, but they swam off when they saw me arriving!"

"I'm not surprised I would have done the same thing if I saw your ugly mug swimming towards me! Aussie added, keen to pay back some of Freddie's humour, it was usually directed at him.

With this Freddie aimed some water at Aussie but he was already expecting this and quickly dodged out of the way!

"Ok guys calm down we still have to get this lot back to land!" Georgi said calming the situation and directing their focus to the task at hand.

"Well, all the water has gone and it's so quiet once again." Pointed out Freddie as only the occasional drop of water was to be heard.

Mikey had already gone below to replace the plugs that Freddie had removed earlier and upon returning they agreed to try with the help of Pete and Andre to continue to the land with the fish.

So, with an agreement reached Andre lowered the Botmobile back into the water and moved towards the net in case his help was needed.

Mikey connected the power and they slowly edged forward again.

Brace yourselves for when we start pulling the net." Mikey advised, to get everyone ready for the large jolt they experienced last time. The guys, Pete and Andre swam alongside as the remaining occupants of the Botmobile felt the sudden tug as the full weight of the net was taken up by the Botmobile but this time they were ready for it, but it was considerably smaller.

They gradually built-up speed but there was not the same reaction that they experienced the first time. Mikey was correct, earlier they had scooped up too many fish. This also would have been bad for the lake because the more fish that they took the less fish there would have been there.

Although the Botmobile was slowing down as they caught more and more fish upon their return to the land everything else was going wonderfully.

Nearing the edge of the lake they saw many people assembled waiting for their landing. These people must have been watching them on the lake earlier and were very curious about what they were doing and what this was especially as they had never seen anything like this on the lake before.

"Look at all these animals waiting for us!" Alona said to the guys.

"It's incredible! They have all come to see your fishing vessel Mikey!" added Georgi while Mikey tried to focus on the task at hand but blushed anyway.

"I hope they haven't come to eat my fish because I am really hungry!" commented Pete worried that all his fish would soon be gone as the others smiled.

"Don't worry Pete nobody will eat until you have eaten enough after all we have caught these for you!" she said to the others in complete agreement but laughing at his reaction.

"Ok guys almost there but think we will need a little push to get us out of the water and to drag this net to shore if you can do that?" Mikey requested assistance from Pete and Andre.

"Of course, we will help." Pete answered without even consulting Andre!

Andre laughed at Pete's comments but agreed to help knowing that Pete was very hungry at this time.

The Botmobile slowed dramatically when they reached the mud at the edge of the lake. Pete and Andre only needed to push a little for the Botmobile to reach the land and begin again to move unaided, all by itself.

The large crowd of mixed animals which were waiting parted and looked on in amazement as the Botmobile dragged the net of fish out of the water.

There were hedgehogs, young badgers, different kinds of birds, frogs, ducks, and many other different animals which all lived in or around Landon but mainly from the region of the lake.

At last, the net made it to shore, eliciting a thunderous applause from the onlookers as the fish emerged into view. Pete eagerly awaited his forthcoming meal. As the net lay completely spread out on the land, Pete approached while Mikey started determining the necessary reduction in net size to overcome the issues they had encountered earlier at the lake.

As Pete scooped up a large amount of fish Georgi invited Andre to sample their catch, after all was it not for Andre's help maybe they would have had to give up this catch in order to return from the lake, so everyone was now happy.

Mikey was busy removing the adaptations from the Botmobile as the other guys were telling members of the crowd about their recent adventure on the lake.

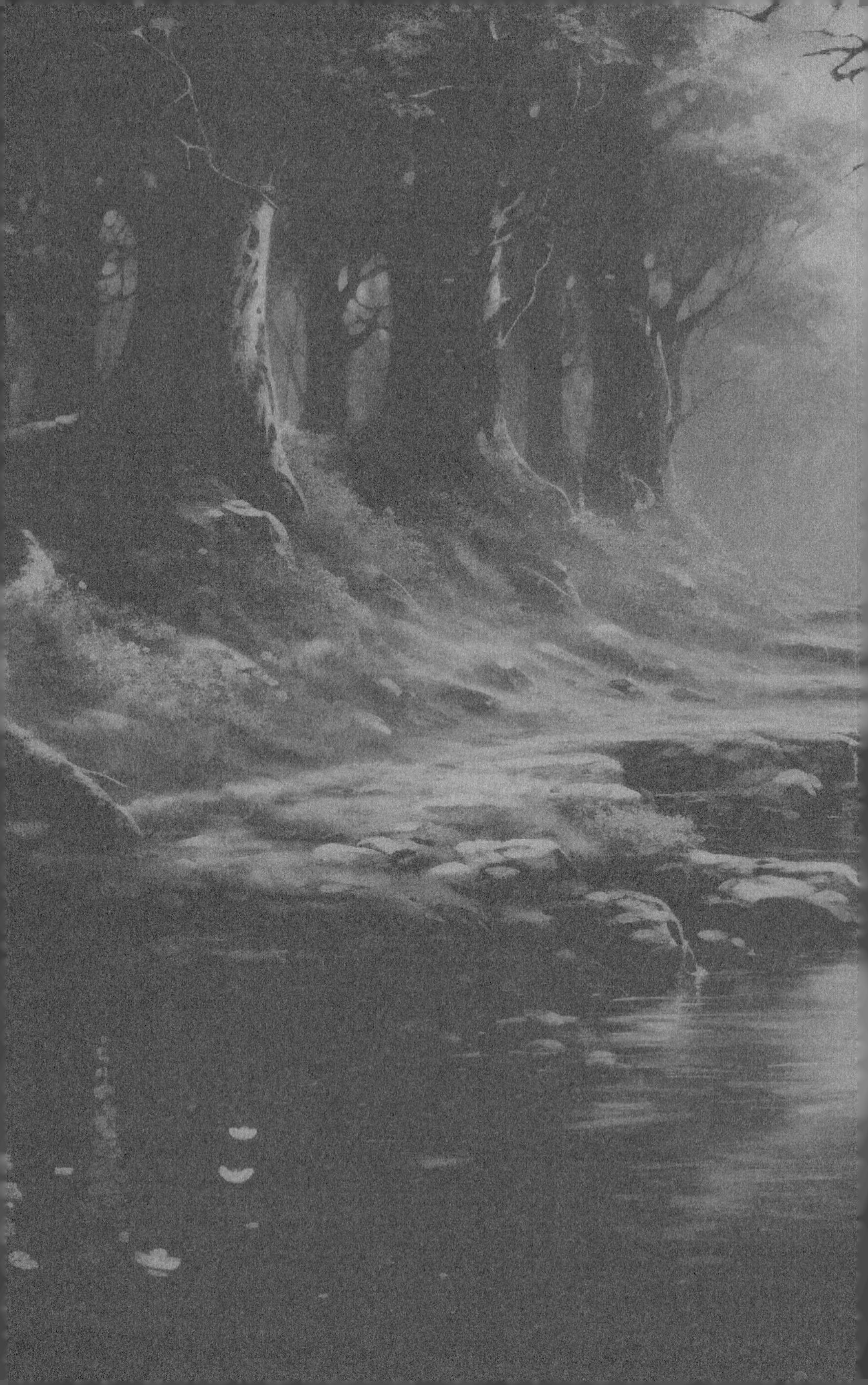

CHAPTER SIX

KIDNAPPED

At this time Georgi began looking for Alona but she was nowhere to be seen.

Just as he was starting to ask people if they had seen her, there was a cry for help.

"Help me please, help!" came a muffled cry from Alona.

Everybody looked towards the source of the cry, which was at the edge of the forest only to see Alona being dragged into the trees by a group of rats.

They all rushed to the area where they last saw her and heard her cries for help but by the time that they arrived she was gone without a trace, no tracks nothing it was like she had just disappeared.

"What can we do now?" Freddie asked Georgi not having any suggestions to put forward.

"We need to speak with Professor Badger, and I think he will have some idea what we can do!" said Georgi hopefully.

"Ok, Aussie fly as fast as you can to Professor Badger and ask him to meet us as we make our way back, Pete please fly over this area and see if you can see anything that is not normal, anything at all!" Georgi quickly commanded. "We will make our way to rendezvous with the Professor and increase our chances of a speedy end to this event!"

So, again Aussie flew off to fetch the Professor while Georgi, Freddie and Mikey set off in the hope of meeting him somewhere in between.

Mikey had yet to complete the removal of the accessories that he had fitted for use on the lake so as Georgi drove Mikey continued to remove them.

After a short time, the guys saw Professor Badger hurtling towards them in the distance and started to turn the Botmobile around ready to return to the place where Alona was last seen.

With the Professor they returned to the place where they last saw Alona and the rats.

"I can smell those despicable animals already but there are no tracks, no sign of them at all! The Badger Brigade will be here later and will search the area for any clues as to where they went from here. What I don't understand is why they took her for what reason?" The Professor was unsure as to their motives.

"They must want something!" he exclaimed, still bemused at this predicament.

"Well last time they tried to destroy the Botmobile and didn't care if we were with it when it went over the edge. At this time, they could have easily taken Alona then, but did not so why I am not sure?" added Georgi also not knowing why the rats had done this.

As the Badger Brigade arrived Mikey whispered to the Professor.

"I think I know where they are, I can hear them and if I can hear them, they can also hear us. They are underground, as a mole I can feel the vibrations of their movements below us, not all of them, just a few."

Half of the Badger Brigade were ordered by the Professor to spread out and search for any clues, the others were quietly told to check for tunnel entrances in this area with Mikey Moles expert guidance. "Keep an eye out for any recently blocked entrances!" Mikey said quietly to the brigade.

"So, what will we do when we find these tunnels sir?" Georgi asked, hoping the Professor had a good plan.

"We will dig them out, Badgers are very powerful at digging and I suspect that these are only small tunnels which will be very easy." He declared, now confident of catching these animals.

"I have a better and quicker idea. Once we find the entrance, we will know which direction the tunnel is going. I can then track them from here until we locate the main group of rats, then we block their escape routes and dig them out!" Mikey whispered, clearly determined to save his friend.

The Professor and Mikey agreed as a group from Badger Brigade signalled that they had found a tunnel entrance. The Professor asked them to quietly determine the direction of the tunnel and then to look for other entrances to be sure that they were following the correct tunnel.

One of the Badgers inserted part of his claw into the tunnel entrance and gently removed the earth as quietly as he could so that they knew the tunnel direction.

Mikey then quietly followed the tunnel knowing through the vibrations under his footsteps where it was hollow beneath the ground and was slowly followed by Georgi, the Professor.

Badger Brigade was instructed by Mikey to stay back as he didn't want to alert the rats to their whereabouts with too much noise from all the footsteps on the ground above them.

Professor Badger ordered them to keep their distance but always keep them in view and to be ready when they were called upon.

The other half of the badger brigade continued to search to look for other entrances, tracks, or any traces that the rats had been there.

Mikey signalled that there were two rat guards in the tunnel below, two members of Badger Brigade stood quietly on either side of the rats' location underground. The plan was simple, when the others were far enough away, they would collapse the tunnel at both sides thereby trapping the rats below in the remaining section of the tunnel. After a short time, they then expected the rats to dig themselves out, if they did not try to exit but to wait it out, they would collapse the remaining part of the tunnel also and retrieve them this way.

The main group moved further away, one of the badgers put his ear to the ground and upon hearing them below he signalled the other to move into position.

Quietly but quickly, they moved into position, together with one huge stamp they collapsed the tunnel trapping the rats in the section in between.

Immediately after this the badgers listened for evidence that the rats were caught below them, they were trapped and could clearly be heard panicking below them.

Now they would wait for a short time hoping the rats would appear by digging themselves out. If they did not, the Badger Brigade had orders to collapse the remaining section so that the rats would never leave this place.

Meanwhile up ahead, Mikey was continuing to follow the tunnel and the main body of rats which he sensed were not too far ahead.

At last, he thought they had reached their destination, he had found a large underground cave, surely this must be the main nest, he thought.

But there was very little activity, he could only detect the faintest of movement below.

It was then that Mikey realised that there were many other tunnels which all came together at this cave which was like a central point leading to many different places.

He quickly located the remaining tunnels, there were five other tunnels as well as the one they had followed six possible exits from here.

A speedy decision was quickly reached. Block all the exits at the same time and dig out the main central cave after which they can find out which tunnel Alona had disappeared into.

Their thoughts turned to Alona, was she still okay, why were they doing this to her, why had they taken her?

Hopefully, very soon these and other questions will be answered.

The Professor gave the signal and as earlier the tunnels were blocked to prevent any escape.

Immediately after this a group of badgers began digging furiously to reveal the large cave below.

The Professor moved the guys a safe distance as the dirt flew everywhere in all directions as their huge claws ripped through the earth with incredible speed.

Unfortunately, the only rat occupant that they found had been crushed as they blocked the exit tunnels, but all was not lost.

Georgi believed that he could find Alona's scent because all animals have a unique smell. Almost as quickly as they had blocked all the escape routes, these huge earth-moving machines that were the badgers re-opened these tunnels again.

As each tunnel was unblocked Georgi entered it for a short way to check for Alona's unique aroma. Upon reaching the fourth he leapt with excitement, "she has definitely been in here!"

"Ok, now check the last one!" the Professor commanded. "But she went in this one!" Georgi repeated not wanting to waste any more time.

"She may also have gone into this one so please check it quickly, we need to be 100 percent sure!" the Professor said anxiously.

Georgi quickly checked the last tunnel and was pleased to announce that she hadn't been there.

Now they knew they were on the right track, Mikey quickly started tracing the destination of the tunnel while the Badger Brigade dealt with a further two rat guards in the tunnels along the way.

After about twenty-five minutes, Mikey sighed, "Oh No! The tunnel ends here. This is the tunnel exit; they are not underground anymore. Everyone rushed to Mikey's position and peered at the opening in front of them that was where the rats had exited the tunnel.

"Aussie, take a look from the sky!" Georgi commanded, hoping that they could be seen somewhere ahead.

But Aussie was already airborne climbing high into the blue sky above them.

The Professor ordered the Badger Brigade to check for any tracks, traces, anything that could give them a clue as to where the rats were going.

"Sir we have found some tracks, they left here in some kind of machine and headed in that direction!" he advised pointing to the region where they had gone.

Aussie now returned, "There is a dust cloud way off in the distance that could be them because I saw nothing else! It's heading towards Rat City, but I am not sure if it is them or not." He reported.

"Follow them Aussie and see if you can get close enough to see if it is them or not! If it is them, when they stop, return, and tell us their location and we will now head in the same direction until we hear from you!" the Professor commanded.

Aussie took to the skies once again. "As quick as you can Aussie!" Georgi asked.

"I know, don't worry we will find her!" as he disappeared beyond the treetops.

Professor Badger instructed the Badger Brigade to carry Georgi's friends as he once again lifted Georgi onto his shoulders.

"If they go to Rat City, how will we get her back?" Georgi asked fearing the worst.

"I don't think that they are going there but I do believe they have somewhere not so far away from that City, and they wouldn't want to be too far from their kind. Whether the King has located their whereabouts I hope so." Professor Badger told Georgi.

"At least now we know why many animals sensed something, not correct at Landon these last few days, but could see nothing as they were hiding in these tunnels." He said solving one mystery but not the mystery that Georgi wanted him to solve.

The badgers set off at blistering pace with Freddie and Mikey now experiencing what Georgi had the last time that he went to Rat City.

They were moving so fast that they were bouncing uncontrollably, clinging desperately to the badgers below them as they thundered through the forest like a Bat out of hell.

"Sorry for the bumpy ride," the Professor shouted, "but we have a lot of ground to cover if we are to catch up with them!" he added as they had very little time to view their surroundings as they were too busy focusing on holding on.

The forest was very quiet with only the sound of the rushing Badger Brigade, which was occasionally broken by the noise of plants brushing against the badgers.

After what seemed like a lifetime, they suddenly slowed down their pace, Aussie had signalled from above. They stopped and Aussie flew down to them very eager to tell the Professor his information, "The rebels are up ahead, there is a huge number of them. Pete joined me in the search and is now flying above so that I can lead you there. I haven't seen Alona, I thought I heard her voice once but couldn't be sure if she was there with them or not!" Aussie informed them looking tired but eager to continue in finding his friend as he pointed in the direction of the rats.

With this information they charged ahead and after a few short minutes reached their destination.

Then Professor Badger saw Alona ahead of them, tied to a tree but as they moved closer, they could see that Alona was shaking her head to say no, something was wrong.

As they stopped the Professor inadvertently set off some kind of booby trap.

Whoosh! A spear went hurtling towards Alona and embedded itself in the tree above her head!

The Professor ordered everyone to freeze where they were standing in order to avoid activating any further booby traps.

As they did so the sound of loud laughter filled the air up ahead in the distance, the rebels were enjoying this.

"Right, without moving, everyone looks around you, see if you can see anything out of the ordinary, if you cannot drop down on your knees and check the forest floor around you. Mark anything unusual so that everyone can avoid it!" instructed the Professor.

"Aussie fly to Alona and untie her but she must stay there!" he then bellowed.

There were so many trip wires but many of them were not connected to any traps they were just duds!

"Please be careful, they laid many booby traps here!" Alona shouted when Aussie untied her gagged mouth.

"Professor, maybe Pete can swoop down here and carry Alona to safety? Mikey suggested.

"Good idea! Aussie when you have finished untying Alona ask Pete if he can fly down and lift Alona out of this area, you sit down, stay still, and wait for my command!" he added, addressing Alona who nodded in agreement.

When Aussie had freed Alona, he flew once again into the skies to fetch Pete reminding her to sit still and wait a little longer.

Before Aussie could return with Pete there was another loud "Whoosh" a second trap had been activated. The spear again struck the tree very close to the first one with a loud thud followed by a thwack as it vibrated in the tree but fortunately Alona was well clear at this point.

"Be careful men!" The Professor shouted not knowing where the next spear would go. Aussie flew back down, checked the ground close to Alona to ensure that it was without booby traps, then he instructed her where to stand and told her to join her hands together above her head as Pete could not risk landing near to her. "We don't want him to set off any more traps now do we?" we said in his concerned voice.

Alona did as he instructed and within seconds of doing so Pete swooped down towards her.

"Just hold on tight, keep your hands together and he will lift you up to take you out of here!" Aussie instructed while watching Pete descend ever closer to Alona.

Pete's beak entered the opening in Alona's clasp arms and lifted her clear of the forest floor; he then slowly turned and released her behind her waiting friends.

Pete's landing triggered a large number of whooshes, followed by thwacks as many more booby traps were set off.

"This seems almost like some kind of a game they obviously knew we would come and somehow knew we were coming." He said trying to figure out why this was happening.

"From what I understand they were expecting this but hoped they would successfully escape.

But they knew you were coming and that you were very close!" Alona informed the Professor and his General.

But how did they know where we were?" asked the General, curious that such small creatures had eluded them somehow.

Alona answered. "They have some spies in the trees, constantly giving information on your whereabouts so both them and I knew you were coming!" she said with a huge smile. "Thank you so much to all of you, for saving me!" she added, tearfully relieved that this was finally over.

"You are a sight for sore eyes," said Georgi, happy that Alona was finally safe and back with the gang.

"And thanks to you Alona that I could ride like the wind on the back of a badger to come to your rescue, it was incredible!" Freddie said, his humour showing the happiness that all was now much better.

Everyone laughed as the tension quickly faded away with the relief that Alona was safe.

"Right! Now down to more serious business! By the time we clear all of these booby traps the rats will be long gone and I think you have had enough excitement for one day, so now we should return to Landon." The Professor said, needing to return them to the safety of their homes.

"But what will we do about the rats?" Georgi asked.

"I'll send a small scouting party to follow them, maybe they will get lucky, but I doubt it, but who knows!" Professor Badger answered even more eager to rid Landon of this rat plague that was obviously growing.

"I will also send a small group to Rat City, they can accompany the scouting party as far as they can then confer with the King because I need to be sure this is not his doing!" The Professor added, keen to get to the bottom of all of this.

So, after consulting the General, two small parties of Badgers retreated a short distance to go around the booby trap area to continue their pursuit of the culprits.

Whoosh! A third spear headed for the tree where Alona was tied to earlier.

"The strange thing was that every time one of the booby traps went off, I'm sure that I saw a glimmer of light in the tree above Alona," said Freddie. "I saw a flicker of light once and thought it was just the sunlight reflecting off something." answered Mikey.

"There have been rumours of fairies in the woods, but I think that sunlight reflecting is more realistic." added Aussie.

"Booby traps, Rats, I despise these creatures!" Professor Badger shouted.

"Ok, it's time to get you out of here young lady!" With this he instructed the remaining badgers to return to Landon.

The guys as before were lifted onto the badger's shoulders.

"You'll enjoy this part of the journey Alona, but maybe we can go back a little slower Professor? My stomach is still up in my throat from the journey coming here!" exclaimed Freddie speaking about the journey so far.

Amongst the many chuckles the Professor answered, "Of course we will go a little slower, we are all tired after racing here!" The Professor joined in the laughter while hoisting Georgi on his shoulders.

"Ok Badger Brigade, Mission Accomplished! Let's go home! Steadily for Freddie`` The laughter continued as they set off homeward bound.

Upon reaching Landon Badger Brigade was thanked for their participation, instructed to always be on alert and dismissed to their respective homes.

"So, please tell us the story of the Rat's relic?" the guys asked.

"Don't you think that you have had enough excitement for one day?" The Professor asked, laughing because he already knew the answer!

"But we need to know the story of this relic to try to understand why they took Alona!" answered Georgi eager for more information.

"Let's leave that story for another day, it will be something to look forward to and I said that I will tell it to you, which of course I will, only on another day."

"Ok, I will accompany you to take the Botmobile home and then we can relax, I think today has been more than enough!"

With this they all took a steady stroll towards the lake to collect the Botmobile, but Mikey was walking faster hoping the previous events were not just a decoy to steal it.

Pete had already returned to the Treehouse but had forgotten to tell Mikey that he had asked a few of the crowd that were present earlier to guard it for him.

Had Mikey known this then maybe he wouldn't have worried as much.

Mikey breathed a huge sigh of relief upon seeing his beloved Botmobile standing proudly beside the lake. Andre the turtle was sitting alongside it like a sentry guarding it on their behalf.

A variety of animals were also in attendance, some simply observing this marvellous invention, while others stood guard, poised to ensure the safe return of their companions and to witness them steer the machine away.

Upon reaching his Botmobile guardians, Mikey thanked each in turn as once again Andre disappeared into the lake only too happy to help his new friends.

They decided to return to Mikey's workshop where they would make the net smaller and correct the adaptations for the lake in readiness for the next day's fishing.

The guys completed this while The Professor took Alona home so her worried parents knew that she was ok, she told the guys she would return later to help them with their tasks and despite the guys saying it wasn't necessary she insisted.

When Alona returned, she was accompanied by a member of the Badger Brigade as the Professor had ordered patrols in the area.

The work was almost completed and when everything was ready for the fishing trip the next day, they all agreed to go to Georgi's Grandma's for Cherry Pie and Cha-yorchik.

When they arrived at Georgi's home his Grandma was so relieved to see they were all ok.

"Why didn't you come home first, I have been worried about you all?" she asked cuddling Alona.

"I am so glad that you are safe and well! I hope those rodents didn't hurt you?" Grandma added, continuing to gently hug Alona.

"I am fine, there is nothing to worry about, they did not hurt me, I was just worried because I didn't know what was going to happen. If it wasn't for my friends, I would probably still be their prisoner!" Alona answered, smiling at the guys.

GEORGI AND FRIENDS

"Yes, we all need good friends, life is so much better when we have good friends!" Grandma said, agreeing with Alona.

Sorry Grandma, been a hectic day and I knew that you knew we were all safe and well, but I didn't think!" blurted Georgi.

"Goodness gracious me! Make sure that you remember if there is a next time young man and the rest of you for that matter, now let's have some pie and a cup of tea, then you can tell me all about it!" Grandma ordered, giving Alona another hug before going to make the tea.

"Cha-yorchik and pie!" Aussie murmured to a chorus of laughter from the others.

As they told the story of their day, Grandma sighed and then cheered as the story unfolded, Alona many times almost cried with happiness realizing the lengths that her friends had gone to ensure her safe return.

"Oh, Mikey you were so clever to track the rats underground" and Aussie flying so much, you must have been so tired? She asked.

"I didn't think of it at the time, Grandma!" he answered.

"And you Freddie, enduring such a bumpy ride on the shoulders of the badgers to accompany and support your friends!"

"They would have done the same for me!" he said, smiling at his friends.

"And of course, Georgi finding Alona's scent, you all worked very well together to find your friend and you should all be very proud of yourselves! More Cha-yorchik and pie? You have all earned it" she asked to a chorus of, "Yes please!"

The next day they met at Georgi's and planned to collect Pete, but he was already there waiting so they headed to the lake in the Botmobile complete with its adaptations to catch some fish for Pete who was very excited by the prospect of a fish breakfast.

As they journeyed the short distance to the lake Pete told the guys how he had been practicing his swimming in readiness for when he was strong enough to catch his own fish.

But he said something strange which interested Georgi very much, although he swam in the same place every day, today he had noticed something different in this part of the lake.

A large underwater cave had appeared that wasn't there when he had previously practiced before.

"Maybe it was there, and you just hadn't noticed this before?" asked Freddie, knowing the lake very well.

"It's possible I suppose maybe the water was very murky, but it seemed strange to see this large opening deep below the surface of the lake." He answered now unsure whether it had been there all the time.

Last night there was a big storm and it rained very heavily. Maybe this had something to do with it because you know that water can change the landscape considerably. Mikey commented.

"Tell me where you were practicing fishing and the next time I am in that area, I will take a look." Freddie said as Pete told him the exact place he had been.

Yes, something definitely struck a chord with Georgi, but he said nothing.

Under Pete's watchful eye they again took the Botmobile onto the lake and this time the paddles worked perfectly.

"Great, they are actually going round the right way!" Freddie stated what everyone else already knew but was happy that all was going to plan.

From their position in the middle, they could see the Badgers patrolling the pathway between the lake and forest beyond, Landon was taking no chances until the rat problem had been resolved.

Alona loved being on the lake, looking below through the Botmobile's clear bottom and seeing all the marine life living below the surface of the lake. For the guys to see the lake so full of life below was incredible even for Freddie, who actually lived there because he had never seen it like this.

As Alona and Freddie lowered the net into the water Georgi turned to Mikey and asked about his Botmarine project, "Do you really think that we could explore the lake with this?" he asked curiously.

"Yes of course! It is almost finished but I am busy finishing my explorer project." He answered.

"An explorer project, what is this?" Georgi asked, wondering what he was now working on.

"I spoke with Pete about him carrying the Botmobile to distant places and when he would get tired, we could drive a little. When he agreed, I developed a harness that would secure the Botmobile to his back so that he could fly with us sitting in it allowing us to go anywhere that he was capable of flying to." Mikey explained, excited at the prospect of achieving a lifelong dream, to actually fly.

"Flying in the Botmobile what next you are incredible, absolutely, amazing, a genius! When will this be ready to test?" he asked eagerly.

"It's ready now, I am only waiting for Pete to be strong enough so that he is also comfortable doing this."

"And how does it work?" Georgi added, extremely interested.

"We just fit the harness to Pete and drive the Botmobile on tracks, onto Pete's back. Then we secure it in place so that it doesn't fall off because we do not want that to happen do, we!"

"Yes of course, I understand it definitely needs to be secure!" he said with a huge smile, still amazed at what he was telling him.

"But do you have some emergency system for us to land safely if something goes wrong?" now thinking about the danger of being high in the sky if there is a problem.

"Of course, I do! But I don't ever want to test this!" he said with a chuckle knowing it would work anyway.

"Flying! Do you hear that, Alona?" asked Freddie, the fishing net now in the water and the guys totally focused on what Georgi and Mikey were talking about.

"I have always wanted to fly! When can we test it? Asked Freddie," I have never flown before, maybe almost when I was on a badger's back, but I've never been up in the air before!" he asked, now very eager to fly.

"When Pete is strong enough! The last thing we need is Pete not being able to fly us back or having some problems while we are up there."

"Understand completely!" Freddie answered so eager to experience flying.

At that moment Pete hearing the conversation gave his opinion, "Tomorrow after I eat, I will be strong enough if you wish to test this. Maybe we can go for a flight around Landon to test everything?" he answered eager to repay the guys who were feeding him.

"That would be absolutely fantastic! Flying in the sky, I'm going flying tomorrow!" commented Freddie who was now dancing in celebration of this event and being able to see the world from above.

"Ok, slow down guys back up a little!" ordered Aussie worried about his friend's safety.

"Will it be safe?" he questioned, always worrying.

"How will we know if we don't try it? If anyone does not feel comfortable or safe with this, then they should wait on the ground until we test it and return!"

"Maybe we should focus on getting these fish caught and then discuss this?"

"Yes! Yes! Catch some fish for me!" Pete excitedly shouted, while the Botmobile started forward to return to the land, he took up a position behind the net occasionally checking how full it was.

The Botmobile slowly jolted as the machine took up the weight of the greatly reduced net without any problems.

And without the slightest hiccup, they moved under their own power without any assistance towards the edge of the lake where they usually landed.

"Oh Yes! It's filling up nicely guys!" Pete shouted as he took his head out from under the water.

"Plenty of fish for me!" he added with everyone already laughing.

Nearing the shore, they saw a badger now moving towards the lake and their friend Andre sitting waiting probably in case they needed any assistance but maybe also hoping that Pete would need assistance eating these fish.

The Botmobile was now on dry land and effortlessly dragging the net of fish out of the water, their mission had been one hundred percent successful.

The fish spilled onto the ground. "There's more fish than you can shake a stick at," followed by a very hungry Pelican asking Andre to accompany him with his breakfast.

"If you insist!" he answered, tucking into the fish with Pete.

The guys gave each other a "high five" to mark a very successful mission indeed and then sat down to discuss the main topic, Flying tomorrow!

Aussie was still eager to slow things down a little, wanting everything to be as safe as it could possibly be.

"So, what safety precautions have you got to ensure this will work ok? He asked, determined to ensure that everything was certainly in place for a successful mission.

"The Botmobile will be held onto the harness with four straps, two will be enough but I took the precaution of using four to ensure that it will never break loose." Mikey answered, sure that given the dangers connected with this project that every possible thing that could go wrong wouldn't.

"I will also take with us some replacements in case one is damaged then we can stop and replace it." He added.

"And what will you do if it rains?" Aussie asked believing he had found a problem with their plans.

Before Mikey had a chance to answer Freddie quipped, "We'll get wet! He said, now chuckling uncontrollably.

"Be serious Freddie!" Aussie snapped. "It needs to be totally safe. There is no room for error with this, no badgers, or turtles to come to your rescue! So, it's very serious!"

"If it rains then we don't fly and if it starts to rain while we are flying, we will land until it stops." Georgi declared seeing that Aussie was worried about his friend's safety.

"Don't forget we also have the roof on the Botmobile." Mikey answered, also keen to put him at ease.

Aussie had realised that his friends were going to fly and although he took this for granted flying every day himself, he just wanted to understand that every possible problem had been thought about and a plan of action for everything possible was available.

Eventually after much discussion it was agreed that tomorrow they would test this new method of travel and their new way of seeing the world.

The rest of the day was spent relaxing by the lake and occasionally they took the Botmobile for a cruise around the lake, sometimes just drifting, floating on the water, watching the world beneath, through the clear bottom of the Botmobile.

When the water level inside became too high they simply made their way to land, removed the plug, and drained it in readiness for another cruise on the still, clear water of the lake.

Sometimes they took some of the smaller animals that were gathered at the edge of the lake with them to show the marine life below.

All the guys enjoyed this part of the day a lot, being able to see their little faces light up when they saw the life below, just like their faces did the first time they went on to the lake but fortunately for them this was without the drama that they had experienced.

At the end of the day, although they had a very lazy, relaxing time, they were all very tired.

So, after taking the Botmobile back to Mikey's workshop, home was the next port of call for all of them.

CHAPTER SEVEN

MIKEY'S NEW INVENTION

Mikey said that he had some more work to do, so Georgi, Freddie and Aussie walked Alona home. Although she said that she was fine to go home with the badger patrols the guys insisted and after the earlier events of the week, how could she refuse.

The next morning was perfect for their next project, the sun was shining, the sky was blue, everything was perfect for Georgi and his new flying crew.

The wind was so light, it was almost a breeze that wasn't strong enough to move the leaves on any of the trees.

Pete as usual was always the first to arrive and was patiently waiting for the guys at Mikey's, by the time that Georgi had collected and arrived with Alona, he was already chatting to Freddie.

Like Mikey, Freddie had always had a dream, a wish to fly high up in the clouds.

As Mikey appeared, Aussie arrived and now everyone was so eager for this adventure that they wanted to hurry to catch Pete's breakfast quicker than he did.

They went to the lake as quickly as they possibly could go and upon arriving there, they were able to drive straight into the lake. By the time that the wheels were no longer needed the paddles splashed into action propelling them out into the centre of the lake.

Pete waded out, beside them, Andre's head appeared from under the water beside them.

"Morning guys!" he said, announcing his presence as he swam next to the Botmobile.

"Great invention this is, especially now you have ironed out any problems." Andre exclaimed, happy to see his new friends again.

Freddie and Alona were so excited about their new adventure that they just had to tell Andre who was more than amazed, he just stared in disbelief.

"I will believe it when I see it! How is this possible?" Andre asked, clearly confused and not sure if it was some kind of joke.

The guys explained how this was made possible by Mikey and of course with Pete helping.

"Please tell me, when you go, I want so very much to see this! If only I could do something like this, but I am far too big and need to be in water, but I do really want to see you guys go up there if you could do this for me?" Andre asked, his voice filled with sadness.

The guys looked at each other waiting for someone to say something, when finally, Freddie said, "Yes of course we will do that for you! It's the least that we could do after you have saved us!" he had a very valid point; the others could do nothing except agree to this small favour.

They quickly cast the net into the water and headed back to the land.

"So, soon we will be in the blue sky above, I can't wait Alona, can you?" asked Freddie, now getting more excited as they got closer to the land.

"Yes, I am utterly thrilled with this idea, but we still have stuff to do before we can do this, for a start, Pete needs to eat!" answered Alona with a laugh.

"Oh Yes! Lots of fish for me and my friend Andre!"

"Thank you, comrade!" Andre told him, as he was pleased to be invited to share breakfast.

The fish were now dragged on to the shore and the net quickly emptied, while Pete and Andre ate, Mikey removed the plug to drain the water and started to remove the paddle system as this was not needed for the flight.

Once Pete had finished eating, they packed away the net in record time and headed towards Mikey's workshop to unload anything that wasn't necessary for the journey such as the paddles, net and other parts used for fishing,

They needed to take the harness and fasten this to Pete in readiness for loading the Botmobile.

And of course, they decided to fit this near the lake, where Andre could watch them take off.

When they arrived at the lake, Andre was already waiting at the water's edge, sitting in the water with only his head visible and his body underwater.

With instructions from Mikey, they quickly fitted the new harness to Pete.

"You look like some kind of prisoner all strapped up like that!" commented Andre from the water with a loud chuckle.

Next was the Botmobile, Mikey drove it onto Pete's back as he used his huge beak to control the Botmobile's forward speed so that they didn't crash into the back of his head!

Once it was in the correct position, Mikey began securing it in place using the four straps.

When it was completely secure the guys boarded, Mikey had already fixed some belts to ensure nobody would fall from their seat! The only problem that they believed that was possible would be if Pete flew upside down and he assured them that this would not happen to the delight of Aussie and the rest of the guys.

"Guys you know that when we take off it will be very bumpy, bouncing with every step that I take until we are airborne?"

"We understand Pete, it will be worth it to fly!" Freddie said.

"Maybe it is better to take off from higher ground, like from the edge of a cliff next time?" As long as it is high enough it will be more comfortable for you!" Pete suggested.

"One thing at a time! Let's test this take off and once we are comfortable and everything is ok, then we can try other ways. Ok?" Aussie suggested still worried that there might be other problems.

"Agreed," said Georgi. "But we can look for a suitable place when we are up in the sky!"

The guys cheered while Mikey double checked that all was as it should be.

"Is everything tied down and ready to go? Aussie asked, deciding to fly alongside until they were up in the air and then he would join them.

"Now we are ready for take-off!" Mikey said with the biggest of smiles.

"Ok then here we go!" With this Pete's wings were fully stretched as he began taking his first steps, moving faster along the ground as they accelerated to take off speed.

The guys bounced up and down in their seats and realised that the straps were the only thing holding them inside the Botmobile.

"Mikey! We need some padding on these seats! My bum is already red raw and sore with all this bouncing! Freddie commented finding it difficult to smile.

No sooner than he spoke, the bouncing stopped, and they could see Pete's wings slowly flapping.

"We are flying! Look at the view, everyone below is getting smaller and smaller like tiny little ants!" Alona observed in total amazement while they were still climbing higher.

"I think we are high enough for our first test flight!" Aussie stated, wanting to make some safety checks so they could comfortably continue.

"Is everything comfortable with you Pete?" he asked.

"All is good, the harness is a really good fit and you guys don't weigh as much as I expected you to do, so for me everything is fine." He answered, pleased with the test so far.

"And how are you guys, is all ok?"

"My backside is bright red! It looks like my father was beating it all morning! Freddie said followed by a loud chuckle. "But it was worth it!" he added.

"Sorry Freddie but if that was the only problem that I didn't think about, I will be the happiest here!" Mikey answered with a wry smile.

"It's the most wonderful thing that has ever happened to me! Thank you so much!" squealed Alona, the warm wind pleasantly blowing in her face.

"Exhilarating! Words cannot describe how good it feels! Plus, it's rather amusing that it is Freddie who is now the butt of the jokes. Sorry Freddie but it makes a refreshing change!"

"I've checked everything many times, all is fantastic so now we can relax and enjoy the ride!" said Mikey, pleased that everything was going to plan.

"So, where do you want to go now guys? Pete asked.

"Can we fly over the lake? Alona asked.

"Are we ready for this?" Aussie wondered.

"Yes of course, if you can double check the straps on the harness and those holding us to be doubly sure?" Mikey answered keen to please Aussie and continue their flight.

As Aussie checked the straps the rest of the guys smiled at each other and continued to enjoy the spectacular view below and around them.

Aussie signalled that everything was fine.

Great idea! And if we have any problems Pete can easily land there!" came the reply from a still worried safety conscious Aussie.

"Will probably be the best place to land with no obstacles and a lot less bumpy!" suggested Pete.

With this, Aussie flew on board and sat beside Alona, Pete slowly turned right to the lake and although the guys were still safely strapped in, they were very grateful for the seat belts as the force of the turn pulled them to that side of the Botmobile.

But Aussie didn't wear a seat belt after all he could fly and felt that he did not need one.

He clung to anything he could grab with his claws, they felt like they were floating in midair but as Pete quickly descended down to the water, Aussie decided it was safer for him to fly.

He jumped from the Botmobile but didn't think about the force of the wind because of the speed that Pete was flying at.

Bang! "Oh my God, Aussie, Aussie hit his head on the roof of the Botmobile!" Alona screamed.

"He's falling! What are we going to do?"

"Pete! Georgi shouted. "Aussie's hurt! He's not flying! Can we follow him to the water and rescue him before he drowns, he can't swim!" he urgently added.

I can do better than that!" He answered as they now descended even faster towards the lake.

"Oh, please hurry!" said Alona, now seeing Aussie plummeting towards the lake but now above them.

"Don't worry, I'll get him!" answered Pete who was now flying with his head cocked to one side with one eye on the falling Aussie and the other eye on the water below.

"Guys get ready to catch him!" Pete ordered quickly changing course.

"Ok guys, let's do this for Aussie!" All eyes were on their injured friend who was dropping closer and closer towards them.

"Georgi, Mikey, he will drop into your laps any second now!" instructed Pete, while Mikey and Georgi raised their arms to catch him.

"Here he comes, Mikey!" Quickly followed by, "got him!" Georgi shouted triumphantly to whoops and howls of relief from Freddie and Alona.

Aussie was now laid across the laps of Georgi and Mikey, "Aussie, are you ok, speak to me buddy?" Georgi asked, praying his friend was alright.

"Is he ok, is he still breathing?" Alona asked with sadness in her voice.

"I'm not sure." Georgi answered while checking for signs of life.

"He's alive! I saw his eyes move!" Mikey stated excitedly.

"Aussie! Are you ok?" Georgi again asked desperately.

"What just happened, I was flying then I was asleep?" asked Aussie unsure what had happened.

"You knocked your head against the Botmobile as you flew." Georgi answered with a smile of relief.

"So, how do you feel Aussie, do you have any pain?" Alona asked in her normal high-pitched voice that she used when she was worried about something.

"I'm fine, just a little dazed and slightly confused that's all." He answered wondering what all the fuss was about. "Good job I was in the Botmobile and not flying!" he said but wondered why the others were laughing as he sat up beside Georgi.

"You were flying Aussie!" Freddie exclaimed but Aussie didn't believe it.

"How could I be flying? If I was in the air, you would have been fishing me out of the river now! So, how could I possibly be here?" he asked, still not sure of what had happened.

"Pete flew below you and we caught you as you were falling to the lake!" Georgi answered and still the guys laughed.

"Really? You really saved me? No! Alona is that what really happened?" he asked, desperately trying to remember.

Alona nodded in agreement with the others as Pete said, "Great catch Yeah! Best catch I have made in a long while!"

"Do you know what I don't believe Aussie?" Georgi said as Aussie shook his head.

"You, out of all of us, have been ranting on about safety ever since we started this flight, and you ignored your own personal safety when trying to fly! Everybody knows that it is difficult to jump from anything that is moving but the Botmobile was flying so you have the wind to think about also and I for one cannot believe that you didn't consider this!" Georgi said, quite happy to give Aussie one of his own safety speeches.

The others sensing what Georgi was doing tried not to laugh but all smiled in agreement when Georgi said, "but we are all relieved that you are safe and alright!"

"We all know how much you care about our safety, but you also need to think about your own safety too Aussie!" Alona said as she gently stroked his head.

"Thanks Pete and you guys! I could have ended up in the lake!" he said as he covered his eyes and shook his head in embarrassment.

"I was hoping to go into the lake to save you! It would give my backside a little cool relief!" joked Freddie to the laughter of the guys.

"Love it when everything works out ok!" stated Georgi upon seeing all his friends smiling faces.

"Do you want to continue, or do you want me to land?" Pete asked.

"Your choice Aussie, it depends how you are feeling?" Georgi suggested secretly hoping his friend was ok to continue.

"We can keep going, I'm fine! Dented my pride a little but I don't want you to cut this flight short on my account!"

"All that is really important, is that you are ok, nothing else matters! Right guys?" he asked as they all nodded in agreement.

"So, now you guys are all ok, I will carry on." Pete said while they floated effortlessly as Pete glided across the calm water of the lake.

It was so quiet and yet so peaceful, like moving on the water but without any sound only the occasional flap of Pete's wings broke the tranquil silence.

Every now and then they also heard the muffled sounds from animals watching from the edge of the lake, but they were too far away to hear their comments.

"This is the place where I was swimming the other day and saw that cave, Freddie." Pete said as they neared the edge of the lake, on the other side.

"I will take a look there later and let you know, I need to cool down," he added, chuckling to himself at the thought of the cool water.

"I am enjoying this so much, ooh my bum! He said laughing at his own predicament.

"Can we go higher Pete, above the trees?" Mikey asked, wanting to see what the forest looked like from above.

They soared high above the treetops, looking down below through the bottom of the Botmobile. Occasionally other birds would fly alongside them, admiring their method of flight and commenting on how cleverly simple their idea was.

"I wonder if all the animals in Landon will travel this way, one day soon?" One of them asked.

"There aren't enough Pelicans!" answered Pete, proud to be the One and Only in Landon.

It was at this time that Alona and the other guys noticed Georgi was staring at the lake.

"A strawberry, for your thoughts?" Alona asked him.

"When we first flew over the woods, below were the badgers patrolling and as we moved further along, I saw something in the bushes, thought it was a rat. I realised then, that when we are on the lake or enjoying ourselves flying up here, we are free. We had this freedom before there was this problem and we must somehow find a way to make everything how it was before! I know the Professor and the Badger Brigade will catch the rebels soon but I just think that at a later date there will be other rebels" he said, still deep in thought.

"But what can we do?" asked Aussie curious about Georgi's statement.

"We could try and find the missing relic!" Georgi quickly answered.

"And how do we go about finding it?" Mikey asked, wondering what idea Georgi had in mind.

"To find something that is lost, you need to know where it was last seen, so firstly we need to talk to the Professor!" Said Georgi, with that look in his eyes, they had all seen before.

"I think it would be too dangerous!" proclaimed Aussie constantly worried as usual.

"How can it be dangerous? We don't even know what or where it is!" asked Freddie, confused about how everything can be a potential hazard.

"I am talking about if it were indeed possible to find it! You know the rats see everything that we do and are going to want to take it from us!" Aussie answered.

"Guys you need to listen to Aussie! If the rats even think that you may find this, they can cause a lot of problems! Remember what happened last time when they forced you to race them? It would be even worse if they thought that you had something as important to them as their relic! I am not saying don't do it, just think about everything thoroughly" Came the voice of their pilot, Pete.

"Ok, so we will make Aussie our Head of Security!" stated Mikey.

"This could be an excellent adventure for us! It would give us something we would need to think about and use our brains!" Giggled Alona

"Guys we are jumping too far ahead! We haven't spoken to the Professor yet! Maybe it is impossible to find this, who knows!" added Georgi, also wanting to know more.

"So, the first stage is to collect as much information as possible and then we can sit and discuss what the next step is." Commented Aussie thrilled about his new title.

"Then we need to speak to the Professor and take it from there." Freddie suggested to the guys, who all agreed.

They continued enjoying their flight, all of them knowing that this would be the first of many aerial adventures.

Soaring over the treetops, seeing their school from above, floating along the path that they took when racing the rats and looking at where it could have easily ended. The edge of the cliff was so high that they could not see the bottom.

"Yes, we could easily take off from here without any bumps at all!" Pete announced.

"But it is a very long way down to the bottom!" Freddie commented his eyes now glazed over with fear.

"No worries, we would be flying after travelling only a fraction of the way down there!" Pete answered with a confident smile.

Next, they returned back to Landon, Pete flew low over their homes, it was pleasant for him to see the guys viewing where they lived from a different angle that they had never seen before.

"Wow! My house looks so different from up here." Said Georgi amazed at how different it looked.

"You need to tell Grandma Hedgehog, that the roof needs mending!" Freddie reluctantly pointed out.

"I am sure we can fix the roof together when we have some time, I just need some help getting onto the roof!" exclaimed Mikey, knowing it was only a minor repair with his tools, he could easily do it.

With their mission accomplished Pete headed out over the lake, gently turned, and slowly descended to land on the peaceful calm waters that were approaching them.

"Is everybody strapped in and ready to land? There will be a small jolt as we hit the water but nothing as bumpy as our take off." Pete announced with everyone ready for the landing.

"We are all ready, unless Aussie wants to try going for another swim first?" Freddie asked then chuckled as he looked at Aussie who was glaring back at him clearly annoyed.

"Very funny!" Aussie answered sarcastically. "Don't worry guys, I'm staying right here!" he added, keen to forget, but also understanding the humour of his previous calamity.

Pete was now flying very slowly over the water; he flew so slow that they weren't even sure if he had landed or not.

With a quick flap of his huge wings Pete announced, "Touch down!" The instant he said this they heard a gentle splash as they landed in the water followed by a slight bump which was nothing as bad as they and Freddie were expecting.

"Is everyone ok? Nobody is missing?" he asked, then sniggered about Aussie, already knowing they were all present and correct.

"I am still here if that is what you are asking!" replied Aussie who then joined in with the rest of the guys laughing at Pete's little joke.

The group were congratulating Pete and Mikey on their combined achievement when they heard a voice from the water, "that was absolutely incredible! I have never seen anything like it in my life! Thank you all for letting me witness this piece of history that you have made!" they heard as they saw Andre beside them in the lake.

"The pleasure was all ours, it was breathtaking!" answered Alona clearly astonished by their adventure.

Nearing the land at the edge of the lake they saw that a large crowd had gathered to congratulate them on their extraordinary feat.

Amongst them they could see the huge figure that was Professor Badger towering high above the animals present flanked by two members of Badger Brigade.

The large crowd parted amidst thunderous applause and huge cheers when Pete waddled from the water with the Botmobile still securely fastened on his back.

"Be careful not to bow Pete! Don't forget we are still here!" Freddie quipped followed by his large comical smile.

"I remember!" Pete answered. "Just soaking up the moment!" he said, turning slowly to position himself for the removal of the Botmobile and its safety harness.

"Everybody please stand back so that the Botmobile can roll down my back!" Pete added, now keen to unload everything.

"Let me give you a hand!" shout Professor Badger upon seeing the guys undoing the straps securing everything.

Upon climbing back into the Botmobile the Professor slowly rolled the Botmobile backwards until it was safely on the ground and then proceeded to unfasten the harness from Pete.

When this was done Pete surprisingly started walking away from the crowd of people.

"Where are you going Pete?" asked Mikey wondering what had happened.

"One second!" answered Pete stretching his wings and flapping. "Just getting comfortable and didn't want to blow people over in doing so." He said now waddling his way back to the group.

"You never cease to amaze me! It is not every day that a teacher looks to the skies and sees his cleverest pupils flying on the back of a pelican! Incredible! I am assuming that this is your work young Mikey Mole?" he asked, completely amazed at what he had seen.

"Yes Sir! It has always been my dream to fly!" Mikey answered slightly embarrassed at his popularity.

"Tell me, how was it, what did you see up there, how did you come up with this idea?" many questions he asked anxious to know about their experience.

When the guys started telling the story of their voyage Georgi took the opportunity to speak with The Professor about the rat problem.

"Whatever this relic is that is so important to them I think me, and the guys can find it and I would like your permission to search for this by gathering all the information that we have available." He stated.

"And what makes you think that you can find what many have been searching for since the day of this disaster?" he asked wondering if there would be any problems if he allowed him to do this.

"Everybody in Landon wants an end to this problem, you said yourself, we are your brightest pupils plus you have already seen what we have been able to achieve together. To start with, we just want to gather all the details that we can and see if we can find something that we can investigate further." Georgi replied wanting so much to be given a chance to end this once and for all.

"Ok, but understand you are my pupils, and I am responsible for your safety. I will agree but only if you keep me in the loop at every stage of your investigation, agreed?" The Professor answered, informing Georgi that this needed to be done on his terms.

"Agreed! But to gather all the necessary information can you tell us the history regarding the events leading up to this?" Georgi said like a dog with a bone and not wanting to let go.

"After we are finished here, I will tell you the story just like I said I would." The Professor quickly answered.

"We can go to my Grandma's for Cherry Pie and Cha-yorchik!" exclaimed Georgi excited about telling Grandma of their adventure but also eager to hear Professor Badger's story.

Rejoining the guys, they were just in time to hear Freddie still complaining about his sore behind.

Telling everyone gathered there how he had almost forgotten about it in the excitement of actually flying and to the moans of the rest of the guys was still going on about it.

"Well, I think that is enough talk about your sore backside for one day Freddie, I think we should head for Grandma's for some refreshments, that is unless your too sore for Cherry Pie and Cha-yorchik?" Georgi asked, wanting even more to hear the story of the rat's demise.

"Oh but of course!" Freddie replied quickly, "I am sure I can endure the pain a little longer and suffer in silence for some delicious Cherry Pie!" he said.

"You suffer in silence? That will be the day!" Georgi responded as everyone burst into howls of laughter.

With this they climbed aboard the Botmobile, said goodbye to the remaining crowd of onlookers and made their way with the Professor to Georgi's Grandma's.

On the way home Georgi told the guys of his conversation with Professor Badger and how when they arrived at his home, he was going to tell them the story of the rat relic.

"What an interesting day this is turning out to be!" Aussie said also curious to hear this story.

Upon arriving there Georgi smiled to himself seeing the curtain move that told him she was watching patiently for their return.

By the time that they had stopped she was already waiting for them at the door, "I've put the kettle on!" she shouted making her way towards them.

"Always a pleasure to see you here too, Professor." She said, proud of the interest in her Grandson. "Hope you will join us for tea?" she asked, flashing her loving smile his way.

"Would be delighted!" answered the Professor whilst stopping Georgi from telling her that he had already invited him there.

Grandma and Alona disappeared into Georgi's home and returned a few minutes later with Cha-yorchik and something to eat.

"So, you have been flying?" Grandma asked, wondering when Georgi would tell her about their fantastic adventure.

"How did you know?" Georgi asked, knowing that Alona would not have spoiled his surprise.

"It's all around the village, it's the only thing people are talking about! Do you know Professor," she stated, "It's not that long ago that I was telling him stories about Landon and now I cannot wait to hear his stories about their adventures. How did you manage to do this?" she asked, curious to hear about her Grandson's exciting adventure.

The guys proceeded to tell Grandma about their adventure that day, each taking it in turns to comment on various parts of the journey.

All of a sudden Freddie asked with a look of discomfort, "Grandma, do you have a cushion or something soft to sit on?"

Aussie leaned towards Georgi and whispered, "here we go!" Then they chuckled quietly to each other.

"Are you hurt Freddie? Grandma asked, concerned.

Freddie yet again began to repeat the incident of his sore bum.

"Oh! You poor thing!" Grandma exclaimed but as she went to get him something padded, Georgi turned to him and asked, "Freddie, what happened to you?" Freddie replied, "I will suffer in silence?" Upon hearing this, the group erupted in roars of laughter.

"I hope you are not laughing at Freddie's predicament. It's not nice to laugh at people who are suffering!" Grandma asked sternly, as she returned with a spare pillow and some cream to relieve the pain.

"It was just something that he said earlier, I will tell you later." Answered Georgi while everyone except Freddie nodded in agreement.

Grandma was spellbound, completely astonished by their story, she sat sipping her Cha-yorchik listening to every word completely mesmerized as the story unfolded.

""As I live and breathe! My Grandson and his friends, the first animals to fly in Landon, amazing!" she said as she went to the house in order to refill everyone's refreshments in anticipation of Professor Badger's story.

The Professor took a deep breath and started to tell the history of the rat kingdom.

"Many years ago, Rat City was a part of Landon, right on the edge of Strawberries fields next to the lake and bordering on the cliff. Teachers here used to teach the rat children and everything between us was perfect, but this was long ago, long before my Grandfather was born.

In these times, Landon had a council of leaders similar to what we have here today. The rats were ruled by their king, who was called King Krooni, but in these times the rat ruler had complete power over all of his rat subjects because he had the "Crown of Hairies". The crown was stored in a strong room somewhere below the city which was heavily protected by guards and many booby traps like the ones we experienced before but the traps guarding the crown were said to be much more complex. Then the biggest catastrophe in rat history occurred, "The Great Flood!"

Records state that there was the biggest freak weather storm ever, which caused massive flooding in Landon on a scale never before seen from that day to this.

It was much worse in Rat City as most of the water was moving in their direction.

For many days it had been raining quite heavily. Days after this sad event, we found out later that there was a lake high up in the hills, one side had totally collapsed, sending this monstrous amount of water, down the hillside and into Landon.

Even now you can still see the route that the water took, transforming the land in front of it, smashing through the land, sweeping away the trees, ripping them from the ground, like they were twigs, gouging the earth in front of it, destroying everything in its path.

The city was being flooded with a devastating impact; rats, although they are good swimmers, were being swept away by the force of the water.

CHAPTER EIGHT

THE MAP

Their homes were rapidly destroyed, whole families were lost, many houses were crushed or washed away, the majority of the rats lived underground, they were hit the hardest, and didn't stand a chance.

The water came with such a tremendous force, a power that was never expected or seen before, there was no escape for them, only the fortunate few surviving nature's cruel onslaught.

The king ran, his only concern was to save their priceless relic, the crown! But time and time again the power of the floods prevented this and, in the end, the Royal Guards were extremely fortunate to save him!

At this time, it got even worse, not only had the land been completely flattened by the river of mud and water, but Rat City also completely disappeared!

"Disappeared?" questioned Freddie wondering how this was possible.

"There was a landslide of epic proportions. Part of the land collapsed into the lake and the other disappeared into the giant chasm that is the cliff edge today.

As soon as the alarm was raised all the residents of Landon rushed to the rats' aid, it was said it was unrecognizable, totally different from before, like part of our great city had been erased completely.

"Sorry to interrupt Professor but please give me a minute as I think I could shed some light on this for you." Grandma said as she disappeared into the house and returned with a very old picture that had been hanging on the wall for as long as Georgi could remember.

"This is what Landon was like before the big storm!" Grandma explained as she passed the picture to Georgi. The instant that he looked at it again for the first time he realised its significance and how much the landscape had changed on that fateful night.

Georgi laid the picture on the ground so that all could see how different everything was then.

In front of them they could see how much bigger Landon was long ago, the map showed rat city in its entirety, the huge expanse of land behind their lake that didn't exist anymore.

"You can see from this that the lake was much smaller in that time and was made bigger by the enormous amount of water that flowed and remained there to this day." The Professor added, continuing his story.

"You begin to see just how much bigger Landon was all those years ago! Thousands of rats were never seen again, everyone who was there desperately searched for survivors, but they did not find many alive.

What was once a city of thousands was now reduced to a few hundred rats maximum, such was the epic scale of this disaster.

The King frantically tried in vain to rule his subjects but all of them believed his power came from the crown which was now lost. Without the crown other rats saw an opportunity to rebel against him hoping to take the power to control all!"

"Like it is today?" interrupted Georgi keen to understand.

"Exactly, like they are today! He was almost powerless to prevent this from happening, most of the rebels came from his greatly reduced army. A huge amount of the king's men were lost in the flood or actually trying to save others.

Without this crown he had no control and although he sent many search parties to find and bring it back, most of the missions never returned and any that did reappear came back empty handed.

The rebellion intensified, a new leader was chosen who led the rats to where they live now, the former King stayed with a small handful of supporters always believing that he would one day find the missing crown but alas he never did.

What happened to him is still unknown, some say he was taken by the new king who did not want him to succeed in his quest for the crown, others say he died waiting for his followers to find it and yet another story tells us that he went looking for it himself with one of his search parties and like many search parties before him, he never returned.

But unfortunately, neither the King nor the crown was ever seen again."

"So, this is how they became like they are today. Descendants of the original rebels will always be difficult for this King to completely rule as most of his subjects do not listen!

They believe only the King with the crown is their real, true, and rightful leader."

"Have they been like this for all this time? Couldn't the citizens of Landon do anything to help them?" Georgi asked intrigued to know more.

"There was a short period of time when things returned to normal, we tried to help by supplying a copy of the crown for their King in the hope of restoring harmony but after only a short time a picture was discovered by yet another rebel showing the original crown and this king was overthrown yet again.

From what Alona said about the relic, maybe they believe that we have it, but we do not!

It is still somewhere under that vast lake, or it disappeared over the edge, into the abyss below meeting the same fate that befell this once great City.

But understand this, whoever has the crown will have total control, the power to restore order to the rat population, to be the real King and divine ruler of the rats.

So, to answer your question, since that day we have not played any part in the rats' problems!

Every few years trouble flares but always these problems are in Rat City without any problems to us, that is until now!

I understand why my Grandfather said it was wrong to just sit back and do nothing unless it interfered with our lives here in Landon.

"It was a problem that was just waiting to happen. It was only a matter of time before the rats created problems for us!" he often said, followed by, "You mark my words young badger, it will happen one day, just you be ready for it!"

"Are we ready for it?" Georgi asked.

"I think so, I hope so, but life is so much better without problems like these." The Professor answered with a sad look in his eyes.

"So, there you have it, a short history lesson about the missing crown relic and the enormous power that comes with it. Life would have been so much better if the King had found it then everything would be normal just like it was before! Now you know the story of the demise of the rats, tell me what you plan to do about it?" The Professor asked curiously.

"We want to collect as much information about this as possible! Maybe other elders in Landon have maps of rat city? It could be that somebody else knows some small piece of insignificant information about this that others do not know. We need to ask our relatives their version of events and what they know about how things were then. After we have collected all the information together that we can possibly find, then we can sit down and discuss this. Hopefully we can fly over the area, we can check out the lake with the help of Freddie and we can also go to visit this place in the Botmobile to see if we can find any clues or check out any assumptions that we make." Georgi said confidently, hopeful that they would see something that had been overlooked.

"This all sounds very interesting to me! But before you go to visit the sight of this calamity, I want to be fully aware of why you need to go there and more importantly when you want to go. Under no circumstances are any of you, to go there without my knowledge, I will arrange an escort for you if we agree to let you go there, understand?" The Professor asked insistently while turning and smiling at Georgi's Grandma.

"Understand completely!" Georgi answered with the agreement of the others.

"The rest of today and tomorrow we will gather information and when we go home, we can speak with our elders about their version of the events, meet back here tomorrow to discuss what information we found and hopefully one of us can find a more detailed picture of Rat City and how it was then plus a map of Landon as it is now. It will be good for comparison to see all the pictures together and if we can find something we can always fly over the area for clues, if Pete is up to another flight, so soon?" Georgi asked hoping that this wouldn't be a problem as he was already very excited and had a gut feeling that something positive would come from all of this.

"It would be an honour to take part in such a noble campaign! And if we could find this, we would all be heroes! Pelican Pete saves the Rat Race!" Georgi said, with Grandma and the Professor smiling and the guys laughing loudly.

The guys went off to discover as much as they could about the calamity that befell the rats.

"Thank you so much for the Cherry pie and Cha-yorchik. It was very tasty as always!" Professor Badger proclaimed, getting ready to go home.

"Thank you for the care and consideration that you have afforded my Grandson Georgi." She said with that endearing look that everyone loved her for.

"You have a fine young man that I know you will always be proud of, he is as always, a pleasure to teach and brings out the best in anyone associated with him, somehow, he always achieves the unachievable! This is obviously the huge part his Grandma has played in his upbringing!" The Professor said, also proud of his student. "We both know that if anyone can find this crown and bring normality back to Landon, it will be Georgi! And, of course, with his friends!" The Professor added thanking Grandma once again for her delicious pie. "Don't you worry, I will be with him every step of the way as we both agreed so he is in good hands!" he added, leaving for home but wanting Grandma to understand that he was keeping both eyes on this adventure.

The next morning, they were all very busy even Pete was talking to any elders that he could find about the history of Landon. Alona spoke with the head elder of the Badger council, Aussie listened to the elder owls as they remembered their earliest teachings surrounding this event, Freddie spoke with the elder frogs who spoke of fond memories they had heard of about how wonderful life was before the storm. He then spoke to the wisest toad in Landon who checked all the old documents and scriptures to be as accurate as he could possibly be. Georgi recapped the day's events with Grandma which he found most enlightening and then visited the most knowledgeable hedgehog still alive. He too checked parchments dating back to before this time but the one theme that they all agreed on that drove them on was that everybody that they spoke to wanted things the way that they were before disaster struck their city.

At exactly the agreed time they arrived at Georgi's to discuss what information they had found, nobody wanted to be late such was the importance that they felt just by talking to others that what they were doing was a universal desire held by all.

Each in turn repeated what they had learned from whom they were speaking to as the others took notes of anything they thought was relevant or different from what they had heard.

They had all managed to obtain hand drawn pictures of how Landon was before the Great Flood.

Pete explained the kind birds that he had spoken to, telling them that he was helping his friends with a school assignment. He showed drawings of how it was before and after and with this they could clearly see how everything had changed since then.

After Pete, the others followed one by one, speaking then showing what they had collected, all of them taking notes if they heard any discrepancies in their stories.

But when Alona's turn arrived, she had by far the biggest find, a complete map of Rat City.

Before the flood, it showed the layout of this old city and more importantly, where the palace was. This was a massive breakthrough, the clue they had all been hoping for, now at last, they could find its location in comparison to an existing map of Landon.

"So, how does this help us to find the correct spot to look?" asked an eager Freddie.

"We need to look at the original drawing of Rat City and find some landmarks that are still there, to allow us to calculate the exact location of the palace!"

"There is an Old Stumpy Tree, not far from the lake that is on the map" exclaimed Freddie, excited to find something.

"Good that's one place found that we can use as a marker, now what else is there on the other side of the map?" Aussie asked, eager to play his part in the investigation.

"I have an idea!" stated Alona, put the new map on top of the old one and line it up with the "Old Stumpy Tree, so that we can see it on both maps." "Then it will be easier to check which parts are still the same!" Georgi quickly added.

They overlapped both to show the area with the older map protruding revealing how much bigger Landon used to be.

"Not really sure how this helps us also?" asked Freddie, wondering what Alona was planning.

"If you look at the new picture of Landon, you can see that this is the route that the flood moved down the hillside." she said pointing to the river-like trail left as this huge amount of water crashed through the forest, brushing away everything in its path, as it hurtled through Landon and over the edge of the cliff.

"On the old map, we know that the Rat City Palace was about here!" she stated. "We know this was washed away by the flood, so if we follow the trail left as it swept through this area, this would put the Palace somewhere here!" she added pointing to the map and then placing a cap on the map to indicate the location where it should be!" she said, smiling triumphantly.

"That's amazingly accurate logic! Now if we move the new map in line with the Rat City Palace as well" Aussie said quickly, as he flew to the edge of the map, he took it gently into his claws and slowly lined up the maps again with the new marker. "Now you will see that both of these, the Old Stumpy Tree and the Palace line up perfectly with this clump of trees that protrudes from the edge of the forest!"

"But we still need to find another point that is still on both maps. We have a horizontal line across the map, but all that water left a huge trail. We need a point on the map that is vertically in line with the Rat Palace but the flood destroyed everything in its path!" Alona sighed, now not sure what to suggest.

And don't forget guys, even if we know the exact location of the Palace, it's a very big place!" Freddie exclaimed knowing that they still faced a huge task to even find it.

They all stared blankly at the map the Great Flood had washed away all obstacles that were at that end of Landon.

"Guys, I think we need a break! Sometimes you can think about things too much" said Aussie, realizing everyone was stuck for ideas.

"I Know what you mean, sometimes when I cannot think of a solution, I focus on something else and when I go back to the first problem it is much easier to think about it." Georgi said now thinking about what they could do to take their minds off finding this Palace.

"We are all overlooking one thing!" proclaimed Pete. "Your Grandma's house is in line with the Rat City Palace!" he added. "But we still need another point that lines up with my home." Georgi answered glumly.

Let's all go and relax on the lake, talk about something else to give our brains a rest." Said Mikey seeing his friend's despair.

"Good idea! And I can eat some fish! Said Pete as his stomach rumbled very loudly.

The guys all chuckled at the sound of Pete's noisy belly, as they made their way to the Botmobile. As they made their way to the lake Pete quickly flew off in the same direction, it was already his dinner time. They took a longer route to their destination knowing they would have to wait a little while for Pete to help them to the lake, as they had not brought the Botmobile's paddles to go on their own. Mikey thought about going back for them, but the guys just wanted to relax and enjoy the warm sunshine.

"Maybe we can go by our Treehouse? Aussie asked, wanting to check that all was ok there. "Yeah, sure we can do that and then go to the lake, it kills a bit of time." Freddie answered needing something to focus on.

On arriving at the Treehouse, Aussie quickly flew to check that all was good. Upon returning he had a worried look on his face. "Somebody has been there, don't know who, there is half eaten food lying everywhere and many things are out of place, I don't think anything is missing, but it's horrible when you look, and everything is a mess!" he said curiously.

"Maybe Pete had another accident and moved everything about?" Freddie asked, hoping that it was nothing serious.

"Let's go to the lake and ask him, then we can relax a little!!" Aussie said taking his Security Advisers job seriously and summoning everyone to the Botmobile.

Upon arriving at the lake Pete was sitting smacking his beak together, "that has silenced my stomach!" He stated, thinking that something was not correct with his friends.

"You haven't had any more accidents at the Treehouse have you Pete? Aussie sure that it was someone else.

Pete answered he had not as Aussie explained what he had seen at the Treehouse.

"Ok! Ok!!" Said Georgi, frustrated at not being able to find the Palace. "Pete is there most of the time and I will ask Professor Badger to have the patrols keep an eye on things there for us.

We all know who we think was responsible for this, but it could have been the crows or just a coincidence!" he continued, very keen to relax.

"I don't believe in coincidence." Aussie answered.

"Neither do I! You know what my Grandma says, coincidence is a word which we use when we can't see the reason why something happens!" said Alona agreeing with Aussie.

"But we need to get out onto the lake like we planned so we can take it easy, enjoy ourselves and have a little fun." Freddie said, just wanting to relax.

They all climbed aboard the Botmobile as Pete moved into position to help them into the water.

"Is everybody ready? Pete asked. "Yes, we are ready!" They answered with happiness echoing in their voices.

Pete smiled to himself and started to push them into the water.

The sun was shining brightly on the calm water of the lake, with only an occasional cloud to be seen. All was quiet, except for the occasional fish, breaking the surface of the water. The guys sat almost motionless, relaxing, basking in the silence and tranquillity. Sometimes glancing into the water or looking below through the bottom of the Botmobile.

The Botmobile slowly drifted on the lake helped along with the occasional nudge from Pete's head.

"Ah, this is the life!" Freddie said, smiling at the others.

Just as he finished speaking a head appeared from under the water, "good day to you all, how are you?" Andre asked, glad to see everyone.

"We are all wonderful." Alona replied seeing how happy Andre was to see them.

She wondered if he was the only turtle in the lake because he always seemed lonely when they met. "Are there other turtles in the lake because I have only ever seen you?" she asked, feeling sad and thinking that he was alone.

"Just a few, not many, we don't usually meet that often. Some spend most of their time at the bottom of the lake and others sit unseen in the reeds around the edge. But I am lucky because I have you as my friends, life is so much better when you have good friends!" he answered with the guys nodding in agreement.

The rest of their time on the lake was spent talking and laughing with each other and all too quickly, the water level in the Botmobile increased, it was time to leave the lake.

Andre and Pete agreed to push them to the water's edge and as they neared the shore Mikey started up the Botmobile and very quickly they were back on dry land.

They thanked Andre for his assistance, said their goodbyes and they decided to drive to the treehouse.

When they arrived there, everything was a mess, it looked like a bomb had hit it. Some rotten individuals had been in the treehouse and made an enormous mess.

They knew straight away that the rats had been there, and they had left their mark. A bookcase was overturned, books were ripped and scattered everywhere, and the walls were covered in half eaten cherry pies. They seemed to have eaten some of the cherry pies that Georgi's Grandma had given them for a snack, and then thrown it everywhere. It looked like a tornado had hit. They had spent so much time building the treehouse and repairing it after Pete's crash now it was the biggest mess they had ever seen.

Pete was sitting looking very glum.

"I'm sorry guys, if only I had been here, this wouldn't have happened!" Pete said, apologizing when he saw the looks on their faces.

"It's not your fault Pete, we don't expect you to be here every minute of the day." Georgi answered the others nodding in agreement.

"There's no use crying over spilt tea…let's clean up and move on," said Alona.

"Hurry up then guys, put your backs into it, we're burning daylight," said an impatient Aussie, keen to get back to having fun.

Georgi, Freddie, and Aussie started cleaning the bits of cherry pie and the many cherry stones then set about scrubbing the cherry juice, strawberry, stains that were scattered on the floor. There was almost nothing left of their snacks, whoever did this, had eaten almost everything. Alona and Mikey moved the bookcase back into place and started picking up the books and other items that littered the floor.

When they had finished cleaning, they decided to have a rest for a few minutes and then Georgi invited them all to his home for something to eat.

While they were resting Alona broke the silence.

"I was thinking about our problem earlier while we were cleaning the floor and now, I have an idea how we can find the Palace." She said with an air of confidence.

Everyone stopped in their tracks, their thoughts focusing only on Alona's voice.

When turning towards her they all saw that look in her beautiful, pink eyes, and instantly knew she was about to say something amazing.

"There are three points we can use to reveal where the Palace was, well three and a half if you count the track which was left by the flooding water. We need to fly in line with the "Old Stumpy Tree" and that clump of trees. Once we are above the beginning of the trail left by the flood, we need to mark it somehow as we venture across it." She said confidently, quite pleased at seeing they like her idea.

"And then we just do the same from your house Georgi, brilliant idea, you have done it again Alona!" Aussie said, happy that they were now back on course, to find the crown.

"The second part is easier than that Aussie. If Pete will hover over the marked spot, you could fly straight from Georgi's home and when you are directly beside him, this will be the location of the palace!" she added triumphantly.

"But what can we use to mark the ground?" Freddie asked, hoping Alona had another idea. "We could give you some cherry juice. It was very difficult to clean up from the floor." Aussie replied as everyone's mind was now focused on each problem they faced.

"Pete and Aussie can you hover, you know, fly, but not move, stay in one place in the air?' Georgi asked, remembering he had once seen a Hummingbird hovering next to a flower.

Both nodded yes as Aussie stated, "I think that all birds can hover."

"So, then we don't need to put any markings!" he added.

"Yes of course! Pete flies from the "Old Stumpy Tree" to the clump of trees and hovers when he is over the flood trail. Then Aussie needs to fly in a straight line from Georgi's Grandma's and where they line up besides each other, we have our location! Well done, why didn't I think of that?" Alona said as she smiled at Georgi, pleased that the problem of marking the route had been solved.

"So, we go with Pete, Aussie when you see Pete flying, you set off from Grandma's, fly in a straight line and we will meet you there! Georgi said to an even bigger smile from Alona.

"It is wonderful how well we work together as a team! So, when do we do this?" Aussie asked now thinking if anything could go wrong.

"First, we need to talk to Professor Badger about all of this, tell him what we have found out and what our plans are. I think we should speak with him and if he is ok with this, we can go further on our adventure!" Georgi answered cheers of, "Great idea!", "Of course!", and many "Yes!" from his friends.

"Ok, Aussie would you mind flying to the Professor's and inviting him to discuss this with us at Grandma's and we will get everything together plus make the Cherry Pie with "Cha-yorchik?" Georgi asked eager to speak with the Professor and eat something.

"Of course, I will! So, what are we waiting for? Let's go!" Aussie replied to more cheers.

As they all reached the Botmobile and set off to Grandma's, Aussie shouted, "I'll meet you there shortly!" And flew away to visit the Professor.

Upon arriving at Georgi's, Grandma was smiling as she stood waiting at the door, always pleased to see everybody who came to visit her.

"How is your hunt for the palace coming on?" she curiously asked hoping for an update on their progress.

We will explain shortly when the Professor arrives to save having to repeat it all again!" Georgi answered, entering the house with Grandma to help with the tea.

"So, will there be any good news?" she asked inquisitively.

"Sort of," Georgi sheepishly answered, "we think we can find the location of the palace and we need to check this, but that is just the start. The Professor asked us to keep him informed and tell him which areas we want to look at. So, with this in mind, I have invited him here, to bring him up to speed on our findings and we can investigate further with his blessing!" He triumphantly said, pleased at their progress so far.

Georgi took everything to the garden with Grandma. Everybody was sitting in the sun, eating cherry pie, and drinking tea, when suddenly, the Sun just disappeared!

They all looked in the direction of where the sun was, only to see a huge hulking figure before them, Professor Badger, had arrived! His large, but old frame, was blocking out the warm rays of the sunshine, that was beaming through the tree branches "good day everyone!" He said, politely greeting them.

"Good day to you Sir! Pleasant to see you again" Grandma said, ahead of a chorus of, "Good day Professor!" from his students.

"I've made you some tea and pie" Grandma said as she ushered the Professor to his seat.

"Thank you! That's wonderful." He said as he sat down and then took his tea and cherry pie from Grandma. "So, what have you managed to uncover so far?" The Professor asked, directing his question to his students sitting around him.

"Georgi explained how they believed they had found the location of the palace using these old maps and their method for pinpointing the location.

Very interesting and amazing how well you have deduced the location, but others have also looked in many places in this area, without any success! What makes you think you can succeed where others have failed?" he asked knowing that they had a good answer.

"If any clues are there, they will be underground. We can use Mikey's skills to map the area below ground and the rest of us can check for other clues. We are expecting to create a map of our findings and hopefully this will help us further." Georgi answered, his friends nodding in agreement.

"Very good plan and I can see that there is a good possibility that your investigations could uncover something new, and I will arrange a guard to accompany you to check this. We really need to keep all this information a secret between us. The rats have spies everywhere, they could even be watching us this very minute!" Professor Badger told them. "Everywhere? But how can they do that without us seeing or smelling them? They are not the nicest smelling creatures!" Freddie asked, and then chuckled, while peering into the thickly covered forest behind them. "They find a place in the dense undergrowth, cover it with cedar or anything else with a strong aroma to cover their scent and just sit there listening and watching." Professor answered, noticing all his students were now totally focused on the edge of the forest.

"Unfortunately, you won't see them. It is difficult to see anything there unless it moves! We only know about this because occasionally the guards find their empty hiding places!" Professor Badger added.

"Ok, after this, we will only talk about it when we are on the lake or at Pete's house and if you do not know what I mean by any of this ask us later and we will explain." Georgi said seeing Pete looking at him very curiously.

"Ok, we will talk later." Said Pete, not completely sure of what he meant.

"So, we will arrange for your little outing tomorrow and spend the rest of today relaxing." Concluded the Professor, with a wink of his eye, they all understood.

"Tell me, what does it actually feel like to fly with Pete? He asked, changing the subject, as Grandma gave him a fresh cup of Chayorchik.

The Professor slowly sipped his tea as they told him about the wonderful sensation of being high up in the sky and how different everything looked from above.

The Professor sat mesmerized, as he listened to the wonder of his students' flying adventures. Then out of nowhere, there came an eerie scream! The professor jumped to his feet, almost spilling his tea, putting down his cup he hurtled towards the path beside Georgi's home. As Aussie flew towards Professor Badger, the guys all stood, wondering what was happening. "It sounded like a rabbit screaming!" said Grandma while putting her arm around Georgi's shoulders.

Aussie was now flying above the Professor's head which gave him a much better view of the surrounding area. "It came from over there!" Aussie stated indicating to the Professor the direction, from which the scream came from. "Fly ahead and locate the area Aussie!" The Professor set off like a lightning bolt, racing to strike a tree. The gang quickly followed, although some distance behind him. They just followed the trail of dust left behind him in his wake, as he hurtled forward, following Aussie's directions. Very quickly they saw that the Professor had stopped and was talking to one of the badger guards, who were patrolling the area. As they saw Aussie flying towards them, the guard quickly charged off in a different direction.

"Those terrible rats have stolen some cakes made by Mrs. Rabbit! In broad daylight, too!" Aussie quickly informed the gang.

"Is she okay? Alona asked.

"Yes, she's fine! She came out of her house, saw the rats running towards the woods and then realised that her cakes had gone!" Very strange behaviour from the rats! Very strange!" Aussie said, unsure as to why, they were behaving like this. At that moment they could hear Georgi's Grandma shouting his name, "Georgi! Georgi! Quickly come Georgi!" They heard from a short distance ahead.

Like a high-speed train, the Professor whizzed past them, also hearing Grandma's pleas. "Aussie please go to...!" Georgi shouted, "I'm already on my way!" Interrupted his friend while everyone rushed to Georgi's Grandma's house. The Professor arrived to see Aussie disappearing into the Forest, next to the house.

By the time Georgi and friends arrived there, they found the Professor consoling his Grandma. "There, there! It's nothing to worry about! It wasn't your fault! I think this was all set up just for this!" They heard the Professor say.

"What's happened Grandma? Are you ok?" Georgi asked.

As Georgi spoke, another badger guard appeared, spoke to the Professor, and charged into the forest.

"I'm fine! It all happened so quickly!" She answered. "One minute, I was in the kitchen, but it was too quiet outside. When I came to see why things were so quiet, I saw a rat running from our picnic area. Georgi, he took your maps! I am so sorry! I couldn't do anything to stop him!" She said with a little sob.

"Not to worry Grandma! At least you are safe!" We didn't need those silly old maps anyway! We have seen them and that's enough!" Alona added, as she joined Georgi in giving Grandma a sympathetic hug.

The badger guard returned and informed the Professor that there had been two or more rats hidden, at the edge of the forest, spying on them.

"So, why did they steal Mrs. Rabbit pies? And then, when we rushed to help her, they stole the maps! I think this was all part of their plan and it worked!" The Professor announced.

"We didn't have a moment to lose! We need to check this area, which was the Palace, before they do!" With that he instructed the badger guard to bring six badgers here, to guard them, it would be their protection, if the rats arrived.

Georgi and the gang quickly got Pete's harness and the Botmobile, ready for the journey. When everything was ready the Professor agreed to go to the Lake with them for their launch and after this he would return to Grandma's, until the badger Battalion soldiers arrived.

For Aussie's part in the mission, he would remain at Grandma's and only start his part of the mission, when the badgers had all arrived.

As they arrived at the Lake, Mickey and Freddie began the process of loading the Botmobile onto the harness on Pete's back!

"Why are you in such a rush to go to the Palace site, Professor?" Georgi asked, not sure of the importance of what was happening.

"If a large number of rats come to this site and they will come, they could destroy any evidence that is here, without even knowing it. I want your keen eyes and minds to look first, without those rats making a mess of things." "They could also be a problem to anyone that is here. So, you continue with your part of the mission, and I will go back to Grandma's and return with Aussie. Don't worry, I will make sure guards stay with Grandma until we come back. They will probably need to go on a diet after eating too much cherry pie!" He said with a chuckle, as he set off back to Grandma's.

CHAPTER NINE

SIRUSS

Pete waddled into the Lake and moved in the direction of the "Old Stumpy Tree" as he accelerated the guys saw the "Old Stumpy Tree" get closer and closer. With a few quick flaps of his giant wings, almost effortlessly, he was flying upwards, towards the first point on their map.

Slowly he turned, until he was flying away from the "Old Stumpy Tree" and was now heading in-line with the clump of trees on the other side of Landon.

"If you guys can help can keep an eye on the trees ahead and behind to ensure, I continue in a straight line, then when we cross the Lake, I will slow down, until we meet with Aussie" Pete asked, informing them of his plans.

"No worries!" Answered Freddie, standing sideways and staring left then right, always ensuring they were correctly positioned between the two points.

They crossed the Lake with Freddie focusing, ensuring they were flying in a straight line, while Mikey observed the ground below, for any irregularities.

Georgi and Alona kept a watchful eye waiting to spot Aussie approaching them.

Because Pete was flying much slower now, it seemed as though they were hardly moving at all, but they were. After a few minutes they spotted Aussie flying very fast and very straight towards them. He was constantly looking behind to ensure he was in line with Georgi's Grandma's house.

The only thing Georgi was concerned with was, Aussie needed to fly straight and not veer off, towards them.

"I think I am in line with your house now Georgi!" Pete announced, hovering, and waiting for Aussie to arrive and confirm this. Freddie agreed that they were directly in between their two points, as Georgi and Alona watched Aussie get closer and closer. Very soon they could hear the voices of Aussie and the Professor who was running below Aussie, "keep focusing on flying in a straight line Aussie, it's very important!" Followed by Aussie's reply, "yes Sir I am!"

Aussie reached their line, Pete only had to move forward a short distance to be right above the crossover point. The Professor arrived with his badgers and stood beneath Pete and Aussie,

"Great work guys!"

You can land now, and I will stay here to mark the spot for you!" As they moved to land, they heard him order the badgers to form a protective ring around this point and to notify him immediately if any rats were spotted.

The landing was very rough and bumpy but this time nobody complained, not even Freddie! Everyone was so excited to be there, it wasn't even remotely important. Professor Badger called Georgi and his friends to him, for his instructions.

Speaking almost in a whisper, he gave everyone his orders, "Mikey, I need you to check this ground, Georgi, Freddie, and Alona, have a good search around, I have marked the spot with the stone.

Aussie and Pete, you need to be my eyes in the skies! You need to tell me the minute you see any rat activity. The rest of you will have until then to find something, because when the rats are spotted, we will move to a different place.

"Move to a new location" Freddie asked, wondering why.

"So, that when the rats see us here, they will not know that we are looking in the wrong place and when we are gone, they will continue to look in the wrong place!" answered Georgi.

"Absolutely!" The Professor agreed.

"That is a very cunning plan Professor" stated Alona, who then giggled with the others. "Right then, let's get on with it! Aussie shouted, as he flew into the sky, to watch for signs of the rats approaching. He and Pete had agreed to take turns flying and resting in-between.

Mikey instructed the guys to look for any indents in the ground, where the Earth appeared to sink, as this was a sign of underground activity.

Mikey headed off towards the Lake, he wanted to check something that he had seen, when they were flying above this place, but it all looked so different, when he was standing there.

As they found something its size and location was recorded, so that later, they could piece it all together.

Mikey hoped to get an idea of what it was like beneath the surface, he wanted to construct a map of the ground below them.

Mikey was wandering around looking for the place he had seen earlier when Aussie flew down to him. Pete had just taken over the next watch for the rats.

"Mikey, while I was flying over this place, I noticed something strange near you.

It was like a path to the Lake!" He told him.

"That's great! I saw it too, but now I can't find it, where is it?" He asked, keen to check it out.

"Walk straight ahead and I'll tell you when you are there!" "Okay" replied Mikey rushing forward in the direction his friend suggested.

"There! That's it! It goes to your left and your right!" Aussie instructed him.

"Thanks Aussie, been looking for this, really wanted to check it out!" Mikey answered, relieved that he'd finally found it.

Mikey and Freddie checked and mapped this pathway, from the Lake, to as far back as it could go, he also added a note, where he believed other tunnels joined it.

Georgi and Alona meanwhile, were doing a similar job with what they also believed were tunnels, when they had finished, they had a huge amount of data.

Mikey and Freddie then double checked Georgi and Alona's findings.

They checked and double checked each other's work and were eager to go onto the Lake to discuss this new information, but the rats still hadn't arrived.

"Are you sure they are coming, Professor, maybe they are already here?" Freddie asked, wanting to go to the lake.

They are definitely not here, there are too many eyes watching for them! We should move you across, just in case," claimed the Professor, as he signalled to everyone including the badgers, to follow him.

He quickly moved further away, closer to the cliff's edge.

"Carry on checking here like you were doing over there! Consider it school homework" He said, as he watched the badgers move into their new positions.

Mikey called Aussie over to him, "Aussie can you fly over the cliff's edge and check if there is anything on the side of the cliff, please?"

"Of course, I will, I'll do it now!" He said with his chirpy voice, happy to play some part in this expedition, instead of just being a lookout for the group.

Aussie took to the air and then disappeared over the edge of the cliff. Pete swiftly flew towards the Professor.

"There is a dust cloud heading our way, I think it is the rats, in that stupid car of theirs! They should be here in a couple of minutes!" He informed him,

"Good work Pete, can you fly and take a closer look? Aussie is doing a small job for Mikey! And I want to know if they are definitely rats or not?" "On my way" Answered Pete, eager to go one better than the rats! When you have checked, keep an eye on them, because they do not always arrive together!" "Will do!" Pete replied, as he flew back towards the rats.

Aussie's Mission

Aussie entered the tunnel entrance and cautiously walked forward, his big eyes were useful for dark places. One minute all was fine but then instantly the light from the entrance behind him disappeared. What was happening, he thought to himself, why had the light vanished, where had it gone?

Next, he thought he heard someone say, "Hello."

"Who was that? Is somebody there?

A soft, amber glow gently lit up a small area in front of him and for a second it was too bright and automatically, he tried to shield his eyes with his wing.

Was that a huge, yellow eye he could see in front of him?

His mind was racing, what was happening, was something in here with him, how could he get out. He told himself not to panic, after all the guys knew his whereabouts.

Slowly he turned to make his way back to the entrance where he came in, feeling the tunnel wall with his wing he slowly walked back.

"You can't get out that way!" Someone said, "In fact there is no way out for you now!" it added, "Who's there, who are you, what do you want with me?" Aussie asked now knowing he was not alone.

"Don't worry yourself, I am here! I am Siruss the first." It said with a hiss. "And I am very hungry to answer your third question!"

Siruss continued, ``I used to guard the 'Crown of Hairies" for King Rhandor until the great flood trapped me here!"

"Do you mean that you haven't eaten in all this time?" Aussie asked, then suddenly wishing he had said nothing.

"I haven't eaten properly since the Great Flood, there were many rats trapped down here with me, including King Rhandor! He was a good King, even when he was dying, he asked me to put him out of his misery! But it has been a very long time since there were rats down here!" Siruss the First said, with a sigh.

"The last of them was a very long time ago!"

"But I am not a rat! I am an owl!" Aussie answered not wanting to become his next meal.

"No, you will not be as tasty as a rat, but you are food nonetheless!" Siruss said, as Aussie felt something warm, but damp on his shoulder and then it moved over his head to his other shoulder. A shiver shot down Aussie's spine when he realised it was Siruss's tongue.

"So, you would prefer a rat rather than me?" Aussie asked, keen to avoid being lunch as he felt his tongue wrap around his neck! "But of course! But unfortunately, there are no more rats left down here! The last of the rats was a very long time ago!" Siruss answered, sighing again and then licking his lips at the thought of eating something tasty.

"But there are rats not far from here." We are on a quest to find the "Crown of Hairies" and the rats are always watching us." Aussie blurted out, not knowing what else to say.

"If you could bring some of them down here, I could let you go?"

"I don't know, it doesn't seem right to me" Aussie said, totally unsure about this predicament.

"If you return and tell the rats, they will try to get down here and I can trap them like I did with you!" Siruss cunningly explained.

He was more afraid than he'd ever been and growing very desperate to get out of there and back to the safety of his friends.

"I must trust you. I let you go and maybe the only thing that happens is I starve" Siruss asked, trying to engineer some kind of guarantee.

"Is the "Crown of Hairies still here"? Aussie asked, hoping to change the subject, and hoping to know that he had at least found what they had all been looking for.

"I believe so, but the entrance is blocked from this side, and I cannot get to it anymore, but tell me more about the rats?" Siruss answered remembering how good it used to be, when there were more than enough rats for him. "Are there many of them?" he asked, very excited, at the prospect. "Me and my friends are looking for the missing relic, which you once guarded. The rats know we are looking for this and are spying on us, watching us very closely. They will do anything to find it before we do! If I return to the surface, from the entrance, they will see me. All I have to do is declare that I have found a tunnel that goes under the old Rat City, they will want to check this out! Maybe they will even lower a rope down here and you can use this to get out?" Aussie said full of hope to escape from this predicament. "Get out of here and find all the rats! Sounds like a wonderful idea." He said with the biggest of smiles. "But if I eat you, then your friends will come and after they are all down here the rats watching you will follow! I think this is a better plan!" he said as his smile turned into an evil grin. "But if I don't return, my friend Mikey Mole will start listening for signs of where I am, maybe he is already looking! But he definitely knows that this tunnel is here because he sent me down here to check it out!" Aussie answered now worried that he had put his friends in danger also. "That's even better! A mole will try to dig you out and when I have finished with him, I can use his tunnel to get out of here and find the rats!" Siruss exclaimed gleefully, finding it very hard to contain his excitement at the thought of this. "You don't understand! Mikey will only locate the tunnel! The badgers will dig it out, just like they did when we trapped a load of rebel rats underground!" Aussie answered knowing exactly what would happen.

"Badgers! Badgers! You are with Badgers? I would stand a chance of getting out of here alive!" Siruss stated to Aussie, clearly afraid of the thought of being dug out by Badgers.

"Yes, there is Professor Badger and six members of the Badger Brigade to protect us if the rats start something!" Aussie answered seeing that Siruss was clearly worried by this turn of events.

"So, our common enemy is the rats? Siruss asked, now obviously worried that Badgers would come looking for Aussie. "Do you really believe you can get the rats to come down here, to me?" Siruss asked, giving Aussie a sense of hope, maybe he should let him go after all.

"I only need to go back to the surface and start shouting that there is a tunnel down here, the rats will hear this, they have spies everywhere and they will want to investigate this! Then they are all yours! So, is it possible to recover the "Crown of Hairies?" Aussie asked, confident that he would let him go.

"I don't think so! The Crown Room is in an underground cave, near the lake. The entrance to it collapsed in the great flood, King Rhandor tried desperately to dig it out, but every tunnel he dug just collapsed and eventually he gave up. Over time other tunnels have collapsed and of course there are many traps to keep anything out, even me!" Siruss said, chuckling as he gave Aussie a full breakdown of the access to the Crown Room.

"So, we have a deal then? Siruss asked Aussie. "I let you go back, you stop the Badgers from digging me out of here and entice the rats down here to explore this place for me? Siruss said giving Aussie the terms for his release.

"Agreed, I will fly to the cliff top, shout the guys over and loudly tell them that there is a tunnel down there, the rats will hear this and will investigate at their earliest chance!" Aussie explained his plan to Siruss. "Please don't take too long, I really am very hungry!" Siruss said as he moved his body, and the light once again was visible at the tunnel entrance.

They could hear activity on the ground above them, Aussie heard a faint cry from the entrance, Pete's voice was saying, "Aussie, are you in there?"

"You better hurry before they start trying to dig you out of here, just remember our deal, ok?" Siruss said as they both moved closer to the tunnel entrance, Pete's voice got louder and louder.

Ok, thanks for the information, you have been a big help! Aussie said upon reaching the edge and seeing Pete hovering outside the tunnel.

As Aussie reached the edge, he took a large jump and then flew towards Pete. "There you are! We have been looking for you for a while now! What happened, where have you been?" A concerned Pete asked him.

Have I got a story for you! Aussie exclaimed.

"Let's go back to the others and you can tell us all about it!" Pete suggested as they flew up to the surface.

When they cleared the top of the cliff, Aussie could see all his friends waiting for them, behind them was the Professor and some members of Badger Brigade.

"Guys! Guys! I found a tunnel down there and I think it goes all the way to the "old Rat City!"

Aussie shouted loudly while imagining Siruss below licking his lips upon hearing this. "Not so loud Aussie, the rats are here, and they are already spying on us!" Georgi explained worried that their mission was in jeopardy.

"I'm sure it goes under Rat City, it might even go to the Rat Palace!" Aussie shouted once again, his friends looking at him in disbelief wondering what had happened a few short minutes ago.

"Aussie, please keep your voice down!" Georgi shouted his command, unsure why his friend was putting their mission in jeopardy. "But it is below this cliff, straight down from where I am standing!" he answered. When Aussie spoke this time Georgi noticed he was winking at him.

As Georgi moved in closer, so did the professor who had also noticed Aussie winking.

"We all need to leave this place!" Aussie whispered to Georgi and Professor Badger. "I'll explain everything shortly, but we all need to go back to Landon!" he continued then quite loudly he said, "let's go and get a rope ladder from Mikey's and we can find what we are looking for!" "Great idea." exclaimed the Professor as he waved all the badger guards towards him.

"Ok guys, back to Mikey's and then we can investigate this further! Georgi shouted jubilantly as he received a wry smile from his friend Aussie.

The Botmobile had previously been removed from Pete's back, so he could look for Aussie, so they all climbed into it and with the Professor and the members of Badger Brigade they set off to Mikey's.

When they were far enough away from the cliff, Professor Badger instructed one of the Badger Brigade soldiers to sneak back and observe any activity at the cliff edge and report back to him shortly when they returned.

The Professor then moved closer to the Botmobile and asked Aussie what all this was about.

Aussie explained about the snake, "We don't need the ladder. I was already almost dinner for this giant snake, Siruss, he forced me to agree, to lure the rats down there, to obtain my release." Aussie answered as he smiled, relieved that he was finally back amongst friends.

"I'll tell you the whole story when we get onto the lake." Aussie answered, still visibly shaken from his ordeal. They decided first to take some tea and rest a little but not discuss anything else because of the risk of rat spies.

Once they had assessed the situation it was decided to go back to the cliff and then go onto the lake. When everything was ready, they all finished their tea eager to return and go to the lake to hear Aussie's story. They thanked Georgi's Grandma, climbed into the Botmobile which Mikey and Freddie had already prepared for their trip on the lake then made their way back to the cliff top. Aussie was still filled with a mixture of emotions, fear about almost being Siruss's dinner, relief that he managed to escape that scenario and escape Siruss's evil clutches but now also sadness knowing that any rats that entered that tunnel were doomed because of him. He was also curious in the knowledge that the crown was there but how to get it he was not sure but knew with the number of rats coming into Landon each day was rapidly growing and the need to find the missing crown getting more important with every passing day but at least now Aussie knew where it was.

When they were far enough away from the cliff Aussie relayed his story as they were away from any peering eyes. Upon hearing this the Professor instructed one of the badger brigade soldiers to sneak back, hide and observe any activity at the cliff edge and report back to them when he returned. They decided first to take some tea and discuss a plan of action regarding the cliff edge, but also not to discuss anything else because of fear of spies.

Once they had assessed the situation with the rats it was decided to go onto the Lake to plan. As they were all eager to return to the Lake, they quickly drank their tea, thanked Georgi's grandma, and set off to the cliff.

Aussie was filled with a mixture of emotions he was afraid because one minute he was almost dinner then he felt relieved that he'd managed to escape Siruss's evil clutches, but he was filled with sadness that the rats had entered were doomed and disappointment that he had found possibly their biggest clue so far in their quest for the Crown Hairies.

After their tea they returned near to the cliff edge where they saw the figures of a few rats standing, looking over the edge of the clips top. They stopped behind Professor Badger who was now talking with the member of the badger brigade who had been left to observe the rats. They heard the badger tell the Professor, there were seven rats, seven rats had arrived and joined together, creating a hanging ladder over the edge of the cliff thereby the remaining rats climbed down using the other rats bodies as a ladder and entered some kind of tunnel entrance. But that was just after you left and not one of them has returned the ones you see there are four of the five original rats that joined together to form the ladder.

"But you said four out of the five, where is the fifth one? Professor Badger wondered if something devious was going on.

There was a problem when this rat ladder climbed back up. One of them lost his grip and fell down over the cliff edge and it's a very long way down.

"I think we have seen enough here to realize that using that entrance is far too dangerous and tunnelling would be catastrophic for Landon if Siruss escaped by any means. So, we need to give all of this considerable thought before you go any further in your quest."

The Professor stated, keen to avoid another catastrophe.

"But Professor I feel that we are so close to finding this Crown" Georgi pleaded, already knowing the answer before the Professor opened his mouth.

"Georgi, Siruss is far too dangerous to be let loose, he would destroy everything here if he had the chance like I said, I'll take it up with the council so we can discuss it and decide our next step. Until then, this area is out of bounds until I tell you something different!" He answered clearly worried about the beast below then the Professor dispatched some of the badger brigade to assemble an emergency general meeting.

Georgi and the guys climbed into the Botmobile to go out onto the Lake and as Aussie sat down, he looked at the rats peering down the edge of the cliff clearly oblivious that they were watching them, they were waiting for their friends to return but Aussie knew that they would never be seen again.

He felt sad that they had lost their friends, but somehow, he also felt grateful that it wasn't him. He now understood what his grandfather said about, "nature being a beautiful wondrous thing, but it also had a terrible dark side!"

The guys were escorted to the main path that went to the Lake. Two of the badgers remain on guard to prevent anyone from digging or trying to access the tunnel in any way, regardless of what animal they were.

Upon reaching the path they turned and headed towards the Lake with the Professor's words ringing in their ears, "remember what I said!"

Their moods were quiet, sombre, very little was said as the Botmobile approached the edge of the lake Alona was thinking how she could cheer everyone up. When we are on the Lake everybody is always happy, Cologne thinks to herself. They stopped at the Lakeside and with heads bowed, they slowly started to connect the paddles to the Botmobile so they could cruise on the Lake. As they took their seats then drove into the Lake Peter gave the Botmobile a little helpful nudge. Then, as he waded alongside of them, he asked, "why so many sad faces?"

"Well, one minute, I thought that I'd located the crown of Aries but was going to be the next minute I was agreeing to trick the rats into the tunnel to save myself. I believe I'd located the crown of Aries. The Professor stopped our quest." Aussie answered the sadness in his voice was obvious to all.

"But you know that Professor Badger's acting in the best interest of Landon. Sure, if Siruss gets out he will attack the rats and the rats will flee and Siruss will head to Landon looking for something else to eat. But I think the badgers will dig him out and dispose of him. He's just too dangerous and the rats will soon be trying to find a way into the tunnels for the Crown. But when this is resolved, you can once again continue your search!" Pete said excitedly trying to inject some enthusiasm into the group.

"What did you mean when you said you had located the crown of Aries?" George asked, wondering how close they had almost come.

"Siruss told me that the crown of Aries' room next to the Lake was still there, I was hoping he would show me this, but he said that the room was blocked off and she could not get there since that fateful night of the flood, as the entrance was blocked." Aussie answered, still disappointed at not being able to go and get the crown of Aries.

"If the Crown room is inaccessible, then Siruss can't reach it. If we can discover an alternate way to retrieve the Crown, we can prevent the rats from making a foolish move and releasing Siruss," Georgi quipped, a sense of urgency in his voice.

"Mikey, can we use the map to help us find another way in? Georgi asked.

"Already checking it." Mikey replied.

"That's the tunnel entrance, where Aussie met Siruss and it extends towards the Lake to these 2 places here where there may be something, but all I definitely know is that there is too much rock so it would be almost impossible to take that route. There are other rooms but based on what Aussie said, I believe that Siruss lives in these rooms here, so again, there's no way through." Mikey said while still peering at the map.

"Maybe I could help with that!" Andre stated, but as he said that Freddie shouted "rats spies as he pointed to the side of the Botmobile and sure enough there were 2 rats in the water staring at the map laid across Mikey's lap. Upon realizing they had been discovered they quickly disappeared under the water. "They're even spying on us on the Lake, what shall we do now?" Alona asked, visibly shaken at seeing the rats spying on them. Nobody had time to answer, because, as she spoke a loud grating noise could be heard from below them.

Mikey quickly descended to the base of the Botmobile and upon returning, he yelled, "They're attempting to submerge us! They're gnawing through the Botmobile's bottom!" Just as he finished speaking, Andre declared, "I've got this!" and vanished beneath the water's surface. Georgi and Freddie then accompanied Mikey below.

"How bad is it?" Freddie asked.

"There'll be through any second now!" He answered, but then it stopped, what had happened, why were the rats now moving away?

Andre had taken both rat's tails into his mouth; he then pulled his legs and head inside his shell and was now sinking rapidly like a huge boulder with two rats in-tow. The rats were powerless, the speed at which they were descending prevented them from moving closer to Andre to free themselves and with his rock hard shell to protect him they would not have had sufficient time to attack him.

The guys watched the rats sink deeper and deeper until they were no longer visible.

"Did they manage to break through the outer plastic, how bad is it Mikey?" Freddie asked fearing the worst.

"We were extremely lucky, another second and we'd have had a major problem. I suggest that when Andre returns, we head for land, and I can take a better look from there.

It wasn't long before Andre appeared, "they won't be bothering you again." He stated victoriously.

"Thanks Andre, you have saved us again!" Replied Alona, relieved that Andre was there to save the day.

"Think nothing of it, you're my friends you would have done the same for me!" Andre answered, Andre was always happy to help his friends.

"Before the rats attacked us you said something about the rooms of the old Palace, what were you going to say?" Mikey asked curiously.

"Yes, do you remember when Pete and Freddie were discussing that cave which was underwater?" Andre paused briefly then continued, "well I checked it the other day and it leads to an underground cave. I'm sorry that I couldn't investigate it more, but it was in total darkness. There was dry land, but nothing was living there, I would have smelt it!

It was just the kind of place where nobody had been for a very long time. I also had a look at the edge next to the lake and unfortunately, it is solid rock so unless you are an extremely good swimmer, it is hard to see how you would get to it." He informed the guys of his observations.

"So, Mikey there's only the Botmarine!" Georgi stated his eyes firmly fixed on Mikey, waiting for his reaction.

"What's the Botmarine? Don't tell me it's a machine that tunnels through rock?" Freddie said, wondering what Georgi was referring to.

"It's not actually, it's a marine craft that goes underwater but I've not tested it yet!" Mikey answered, his thoughts now racing, thinking how they could use this to enter the underwater cave.

"But the main thing I am worried about is once we are underwater is if we can float back up because I haven't finished working on the re-floating mechanism yet. These smaller bottles fill with water, allowing us to sink and then we use these magnetic levers to force the water out and it floats" he said, still wondering how well it would work.

"If that's a problem then maybe I can help with that?" Andre asked.

"What do you mean?" Georgi asked, hoping this was the only problem.

Georgi let out a huge audible sigh as Mikey said it was his only worry, it's simply that if your craft is on my back in the water, I'll carry you to shore if necessary." Andre answered, happy to be of help to his friends.

As Andre finished speaking Georgi again turned to Mikey who was waiting with his answer and he or a label which he and his uncle had kicked to the workshop.

"Good, that submarine bottle!"

"Botmarine! It's called a Botmarine!" Mikey said as he interrupted Georgi.

"Okay, Botmarine! Let's take it to the lake and Aussie when we get back to Mikey's, can you go to the Professor and arrange for him to meet us at the lake, near this cave so we can explain the rest of the plan?"

"Okay, but I want to see this sinking boat first!" Aussie insisted, knowing that the Professor would want some information.

"Will you all listen! It's a Botmarine, it's called the Botmarine!" Mikey shouted thinking the guys weren't taking his project seriously.

"Okay, okay, let's go and get your Botmarine and bring it to the Lake.

CHAPTER TEN

FINDING THE CROWN?

Andre agreed to meet them when they returned, and everyone else headed to Mikey's home. Upon arrival, Mikey opened the workshop doors, and everyone was curious why there was nothing there, even Pete, his large head now peering through the double doors. He was far too big to completely enter the workshop. Mikey moved to the rear of the workshop and slowly turned to face everyone.

"I give you the Botmarine!" He said as he pulled a large curtain to one side revealing his Botmobile.it was huge, much bigger than the bottom will deal maybe three times bigger, the clear plastic revealed seating and on each side were smaller bottles. Everyone stood in silence, amazed, while Mikey explained how the two smaller bottles were full of air and that by moving the lever water was allowed into the bottles, causing it to sink. He had stones in the corners for extra weight and they would need to add more at the Lake. As Mikey started to open the bottle screw top to show them the inside Freddie asked the question, "how are we going to get it to the Lake?" He asked, while scratching his head.

"Never thought about that!" Georgi replied thinking that there was always some obstacle in the way for this quest.

"Don't worry," said Mikey. "That's the easy part." He said as he climbed inside with some of the things that they needed.

"But how? Look at the size of that thing!" Georgi explained as he also entered Mikey's latest contraption.

"We'll tow it on the rig I used to collect it with!" Mikey answered with a smile.

"But where is the rig?" Aussie asked worried that the rats had been and stolen it, they always seemed to steal anything that wasn't nailed down.

"It's already sitting on the rig!" Mikey replied, realizing everyone had been so busy staring at the Botmarine that they hadn't noticed it was already on Mikey's trailer rig.

"So, shall we go?" Mikey asked, eager to test out his project under Andre's supervision.

Freddie was the last to exit the Botmarine, Mikey was waiting to close the lid.

"Let's get this show on the road!" Georgi said to everyone's delight.

Mikey closed the door, and they started manoeuvring the Botmobile's bottom part backward to link it with the trailer rig. The process was simplified by Mikey having placed a ring around the Botmobile, which allowed for a straightforward connection to the trailer rig. Once it was securely fastened, Mikey cautiously advanced the Botmobile, but it remained stationary.

"Mikey, it's too large and heavy! You won't be able to pull the bottom!" Alona cried out, unsure of their next move.

GEORGI AND FRIENDS

As Mikey turned off the Botmobile and it gradually rolled backward, he reassured everyone, "It's alright, I've figured out the issue!" He grinned while exiting the vehicle, and Georgi extended a helping hand. "No worries, I just need to disengage the trailer... I forgot!"

They all laughed as they watched Mikey remove two branches that were stopping the trailer rig wheels from moving forward.

Climbing back into the Botmobile Mikey said, "we wouldn't want this rolling out of here uncontrollably, would we?"

"Not something that size! Anyone seeing it would be scared stiff!" Freddie answered, still amazed at the sheer size of it.

Very slowly they edged forward and there was little room for manoeuvring with just the tiniest of gaps between the Botmarine and Mikey's workshop. They could hear the strange sound of the plastic creaking as the two bottles that were fastened onto the side of the Botmarine rubbed against the main large bottle that made up the Botmarine.

"We are clear of the workshop now Mikey!" Freddie announced, relieved that they got such a huge structure from Mikey's workshop.

Their speed slowly increased as they headed towards the Lake. The enormity of the Botmarine as it dwarfed the Botmobile was such that when they passed any residents of Landon, they could hear them asking each other. "What is it?" Quickly followed by, "it's huge! Maybe it's a mobile home that you can put anywhere you want?" Exclaimed one, "it could be, they could be smaller rooms on the sides!" Another one commented, referring to the air tanks on either side that Mikey would soon be filling with water and emptying so that it sank in the water and surfaced when they were emptied.

The group was eager to pause and address their queries, but time constraints held them back. Reluctantly, they maintained their course toward the lake.

When the Lake came into view, they quickly spotted the bloated figure in the distance which was Professor Badger and made their way towards him.

Upon spotting the enormous vessel, the Professor approached them, curious about their intentions. As he neared the massive craft that had been moving in his direction and received information from the group, the Professor slowed down and walked alongside them.

"What's all this about and what the devil is that? Is it some kind of trap for Siruss?" Professor Badger eagerly asked.

Georgi explained what Aussie had said about Siruss not being able to enter the Crown room and announced that they knew how to get to it as he showed the Professor the room's location on the map, which they had constructed.

"This is a Botmarine, and with Andre's assistance, we can access the room through a cave opening in the Lake. Digging down is impossible, and even if we managed, I'm certain the rats would investigate further, potentially creating passages for Siruss to escape. So, this is the only secure method to recover the Crown of Hairies and prevent the rats from unintentionally releasing Siruss during their quest for it! What was the council's decision regarding Siruss, sir?" Georgi inquired after laying out their strategy.

"The council remains uncertain about how to handle him. We considered excavating him, but as you mentioned, digging down there is impossible due to the rock beneath the surface. We also discussed relocating him to a distant, secure location, but they believe he would detect the rats here and swiftly return. So, the meeting was postponed to allow us time to consult with the Rat King, as it would primarily be their issue if he escapes," the Professor explained, his attention captivated by the colossal craft beside him. "So, this goes underwater in the Lake and enters the cave that Andre has already scouted for you?"

"The cave that I've found," said Andre, proudly interrupting the Professor.

"So, into the cave that Andre found, and I can see from this map that the Crown room is next to this cave" Professor Badger continued while staring at the Botmarine.

"Yes, that's it, Andre will help us get into the cave and we'll shortly return with the Crown!" Aussie answered extremely excited but still a little hesitant about entering this place yet again, even though he knew Siruss couldn't get in there.

"I was so much hoping that this was some kind of an amazing trap to catch Siruss but if you can return with the Crown of Hairies then we must try this, at least it will solve one problem!" The Professor stated.

"So, let's get this thing in the Lake!" He added as they stopped at the edge of the water. The Professor with help from Pete gently guided the trailer to the water's edge. Mikey released the contraption that was holding the Botmarine to the trailer rig and after it was no longer secured Andre slid his head under the rear of the Botmarine and started to move backwards slowly taking it into the water. He pushed from the front-end with his massive beak while Professor Badger pulled the trailer rig free from under the Botmarine.

There was a tremendous splash as it dropped fully into the water and Mikey asked Andre to push it closer towards the edge.

"Alright, everyone, we need to place some of these stones inside to ensure proper balance!" Mikey announced while unscrewing the large white lid of the Botmarine. Following Mikey's instructions, the stones were swiftly positioned in the corners. They entered the Botmarine one at a time, starting with Freddie, who dove headfirst only to get stuck as his feet snagged on the entrance's edges. He landed on his hands, wiggled a bit, and finally made it inside.

Mikey asked the guys to wait, then showed them a much easier way to enter the Botmarine. He placed his hands on the top of the entrance, jumped into the air and slid his feet in first, slowly lowering himself into the Botmarine.

"Ooh, aren't you the little clever clogs!" Freddie said sarcastically as Mikey stood before him.

"I simply have more experience than you do," he responded.

Aussie flew in and landed on the edge of the entrance and then easily hopped inside.

"Show off!" Freddie shouted, followed by his huge grin.

Aussie playfully flapped a wing at Freddie before turning to assist Alona in entering the vessel as gracefully as possible. Georgi offered her a boost, while Freddie was quick to lend a hand as well.

When everybody was safely inside Mikey instructed Pete to push them out to the deeper water and Andre was waiting beside them to assist.

The Professor wished them good luck and a swift journey and Pete added, "don't do anything I wouldn't do!" With smiles on their faces, Mikey promptly closed the lid and, using a handle he had affixed to the inside, rotated it to create a watertight seal before they ventured into the lake.

He then gave a signal to Pete who gently started to push the Botmarine out towards the centre of the Lake. Originally, they wanted to submerge beneath the water and journey straight to the cave but as nothing had been tested before they decided to first travel along the surface to test everything that they could, rather than when it was too late. Once they surfaced beneath the Lake.

The propulsion system worked fabulously, Mikey had fitted the same system he used on the Botmobile, but he had cleverly fitted it on the outside of the craft using metal, which was controlled from the inside, using magnets.

"Since I used materials with magnetic properties, there are no holes, and as a result, no water leaks," Mikey explained while requesting that Freddie examine the lid's seal. Freddie inspected the entrance seal, which was partially submerged by then, and confirmed to Mikey that it was completely dry.

"No water at all, I am impressed!" He said, giving Mikey an admiring thumbs up.

Mikey inspected the air buoyancy tanks on the sides, ensuring they were adequately submerged and not leaking excessively. He asked his companions to rearrange some of the stones to achieve the proper balance. They shuffled the rocks as directed until the Botmarine was level.

"Right Georgi I need you to move that lever so that it's about a third of the way across." Mikey asked and then signalled Andre to move into position below them.

"Okay, Andre is below us to stop others from going too deep, if we do then he will lift it up." Mikey reassuringly declared.

"Three, two, one, move it slowly…that's it!" Mikey said pleased at how smoothly things were going. They could all see the water rushing into the empty space as the air in the buoyancy tanks was pushed out and water from the lake below took its place. Slowly they began to submerge, they could hear only a muffled, "good luck guys", from Pete above, it was so quiet that they almost didn't hear it over the sound of the water rushing into the buoyancy tanks.

As they gazed upward, they observed water streaming across the roof while they gradually vanished beneath the lake's surface. From the water's edge, Professor Badger stared in disbelief as he witnessed them venture onto the lake and then slowly submerge.

"Why am I so big? I would love to take part in some of the adventures that these youngsters have!" The Badger General said out loud to the members of the badger brigade that had arrived to assist in the recovery of the Crown.

"Indeed, it appears to be quite an adventure!" Professor Badger replied, continuing to gaze in awe as they vanished beneath the surface.

CHAPTER ELEVEN

WHAT LIES BELOW?

Back on the Botmarine everything was going great, Mikey took his place at the front and was pleased that so far, they didn't need Andre's help.

"It's like being in a huge bubble!" Alona explained excitedly.

Aussie for once was speechless and he was completely struck by how amazing it all was. Mikey asked Georgi to open the valve a little bit further as Freddie advised him that they needed to go deeper to find the entrance to the underwater cave.

Georgi gently pulled the lever to allow even more water into the buoyancy tanks causing them to sink even deeper.

"Not too much!" Mikey ordered. "It will be more difficult to push the water out the more there is in there and we need to push it out to enable us to surface in the cave without Andre's help. Mikey explained not wanting to take in more water than was necessary as the edge of the Lake grew closer and closer.

"There it is, can you see it?" Freddie shouted triumphantly while pointing to the opening in front of them.

"We need to go up just a little bit higher!" Mikey said as he switched off the power and went to help Georgi with the lever.

"Can you push it the other way a little on your own or do you need some help?" Mikey asked, hoping his system worked well enough for just one person to be able to operate it.

"Need help, it's a little bit stiff and there's a lot of water!" Georgi replied, unable to do it alone.

"Alright, I'll assist you! Freddie, can you navigate us toward the cave? Just make minor adjustments but do them promptly since the Botmarine responds sluggishly underwater. I'm sure you understand what I mean!" Mikey requested while gripping the lever to support Georgi.

Andre kept swimming below them knowing that if his friends needed help, he was always there for them.

"That's it!" Screamed Freddie. "We are right on course at the correct depth in the water and bang on centre for entering the cave! Bang on!" Freddie repeated excitedly, while pointing to show Mikey and George, proud of his manoeuvrability of the Botmarine, showing them the cave entrance ahead.

Mikey and George could easily see the entrance, and they both chuckled at each other knowing exactly where they were steering to. Aussie sat looking in Baines amazement at the life around him, "this was just incredible!" He said to Alona, all around him, he could see many different kinds of fish effortlessly swimming beside them, curious as to what was this huge thing below the water. Aussie looked down below them and could see the huge green shell of Andre's back below them. He looked towards Andre's head, he saw Andre smiling back at him and as Andre winked at Aussie, Aussie knew it was just what he needed.

In that instant, he felt confident that everything would turn out well. Sporting a wide grin, he looked up to see Pete accompanying them from the surface, his massive, webbed feet leisurely gliding back and forth. Pete periodically dipped his head underwater to monitor their progress while maintaining the same pace as the Botmarine.

Mikey switched off the power and the propeller blades fell silent as they stopped spinning.

"Why have we stopped? We are not there yet?" Alona asked worried that something was wrong.

"Unfortunately, on this kind of craft there is very little you can do to stop it, there are no breaks!" Mikey replied.

"No brakes! How do we stop? How could you even consider bringing us in this contraption without brakes? Are we going to crash into the cave?" Aussie exclaimed, becoming increasingly frantic as he attempted to get Andre's attention.

"Don't worry, Aussie, I've cut the power and now we are just slowly jerking towards the cave, Andre is aware of this, and he will help us to control our speed." Mikey said, putting everyone at ease.

It seemed to take so long as they slowly drifted ever closer to the cave entrance. When suddenly they appeared to have stopped Mikey started the Botmarine power for a few more seconds and then switched it off again soon they were entering the cave entrance moving slowly into the darkness with only Andre to guide them.

"Keep your eyes open above for when the rock changes to water!" Mikey announced.

Aussie suddenly realised that although they were now in darkness inside the Botmarine it was still light, but how was this possible he wondered.

He was just about to ask Mikey when suddenly they felt a jolt.

"Have we crashed?" Alona asked.

"I always wondered about Mikey's driving!" Freddie added and then laughed.

"No Andre has stopped because we are here!" Mikey replied, pleased that they'd made it this far.

They all looked below to see they were now supported on André's back. In front of them they could faintly make out a rock wall and above them there was nothing, only darkness.

"Okay Georgi I want you to help me reverse those levers so we can float up to the surface!" Mikey stated as he crossed his fingers hoping that everything worked well.

With this, they took up their positions next to the levers.

"Alright, on the count of three. One, two, three!" Mikey counted down as he and Georgi began sliding the levers, while Freddie, Alona, and Aussie observed water pouring out of the bottles. The Botmarine initially ascended slowly before picking up speed. André vanished into the darkness below, and at times they questioned whether they were truly moving, as visibility was limited in the surrounding darkness.

Freddie was just about to say how it took much less time to sink down because he was getting worried about what was happening.

Before he could open his mouth. There was a huge splash, the Botmarine lurched upwards and then back down and it was bobbing up and down in the darkness.

"What's happening Mikey?" Alona asked, never experiencing anything like this before.

"I think we've just arrived!" Mikey's muffled reply came as she pushed his face to the clear plastic's side to try and get a better look at what was happening. For a short while they could hear the sound of the water cascading and then they realised it was water running down from the top of the Botmarine and they were no longer submerged beneath the water. Slowly as the waters stopped running down the sides, they started to make out the area around them and Andre appeared beside them.

"Why so light in here, there was no light at all. The last time I was here?" Andre asked, curious as to what was happening.

"It's the fireflies I keep them at home, look after them and when I need light I put them into these containers," he said pointing to the four corners of the Botmarine.

"Impressive idea, now where do you need to go?" Andre asked.

"So, not only does this lack brakes, but we also need Andre to guide us since there's no steering?" Aussie exclaimed, concerned that they were taking an excessive number of risks.

"To steer it, I would need two more propellers one on the left and one on the right side, but because we needed to do this quickly, I didn't have time to fit these, but it's okay, it's safe with Andres help. Mikey replied not impressed with the criticism.

"Can you push the front end to exit there? "" Mikey asked Andre while pointing to where he wanted it to go.

Andre looked in the direction Mikey indicated and yelled, "Alright!" before gently guiding the Botmarine toward that spot. Once they stopped, they could see the edge of the rock just above the bottom of the Botmarine at the front. Mikey approached the door and began unscrewing the top. As he opened it, he said to Georgi, "I believe you should go first. Take that string/twine, fasten it to the Botmarine, and secure it tightly to something else to prevent drifting—it's our only way back! Aussie and Freddie, please grab three of those containers with fireflies and leave one at the corner so we can see our way back!" Mikey instructed.

"When we exit, Aussie, can you see better in the dark? The majority of us can explore a bit, but don't wander too far!" Georgi stated, curious about where this cave led.

"Okay," Aussie replied.

"And watch out for snakes!" Freddie Joked but nobody laughed, Alona looked at him and scowled.

"I was only joking, stay focused everyone. We need our wits about us, we don't know anything about this place!" Georgi commanded, stressing the importance of why they were there. Georgi took the twine and climbed out of the bop Marine and was quickly followed by Mikey and Aussie who flew off to explore the cave.

Mikey aided Alona in exiting, and they both took on the role of carrying the lights as Mikey directed. Fred disembarked, and Georgi secured the twine around the Botmarine entrance before enlisting

Freddy's aid in fastening it around a massive boulder they had discovered.

Alona remarked on the musty, abandoned odour of the location, indicating that nobody had visited in quite some time.

The Botmarine was finally secured, Andre commented how everything worked so well that they almost didn't need his help, except for guiding the steering a little.

"Don't speak too soon, you may jinx it!" Freddie said excited at the prospect of exploring this cave.

As everyone started laughing, Aussie returned.

"There's a long passageway down there, but where it leads to, I'm not sure, I think there are a few doorways there, but they are blocked with stone but I'm not completely sure because there is no light at all. There!" Aussie said, also eager to explore further.

Andre stated that he would remain behind to protect the Botmarine, not that he believed anyone would be in the vicinity, but just in case.

The guys thanked Andre, picked up the light jars and followed Aussie into the passage. Upon reaching the passage entrance Mikey suggested that they stop and let Aussie fly ahead, but this time with a light jar so that he could see all that there was, because maybe there are some ratty traps.

"What's ratty traps?" Freddie asked, confused.

"They're like booby traps but made by rats!" Mikey replied as he handed Aussie the light jar and began examining the ground before them. The group gazed in astonishment as the excitement grew with each step deeper into the passage illuminated before them. When Aussie reached the passage's end, he noticed a doorway to his right, obstructed by a massive stone that appeared deliberately positioned to block entrance. Aussie was confident that this was where the Crown was located. He discovered an old, rusted hook protruding from the wall and hung the light jar on it before promptly turning to retrace his steps toward his companions. As he did, he noticed numerous small openings in the walls. Something didn't seem quite right.

"Nobody moves!" He shouted. "Rat traps, rat traps everywhere!"

Everyone shuddered and instantly took a step back.

"How do you know?" Mikey asked, wanting as much information as possible.

Aussie told him about the strange holes in the walls and that there were lots of them.

"So, here's what we'll do guys, stand back and I'll clear the area for us!" Georgi commanded.

They all retreated to the entrance. Georgi walked back further from his friends.

"What are you going to do?" Alona asked.

"You'll see" Georgi's reply as he started running towards them. As he reached the entrance, he quickly rolled himself into a ball and rolled down the corridor faster and faster the further he went like a bowling ball going like a bullet from a gun.

As he rolled along the floor, they could hear the sound of thousands of tiny darts fizzing through the air in front of them. Almost as fast as they appeared they were all gone, all that remained was a corridor filled with a cloud of dust which was disturbed as the darts flew.

"Are you alright, Georgi?" inquired the group, unable to see their friend due to the enormous cloud of dust. "Everyone, remain where you are. I'm fine. I found something. Come have a look and see if there's anything nearby," Georgi responded. He examined his surroundings but found nothing. "There's nothing here. These traps were likely set up to prevent anyone from entering this way," Aussie explained.

"Okay, stand still while I pull this lever! Here we go" Georgi replied as he pulled down on the lever in front of him.

Georgi pulled the lever outward, producing a clunking sound, and suddenly the stone door began to move. The loud grinding noise continued as the stone blocking the opening in the floor began to shift. Georgi peered into the room but could see nothing in the darkness.

"Okay, I'll roll back to you to make sure there are no more traps!" Georgi said, then running forwards, jumping into a ball and spinning back towards where they were standing.

He stood up triumphantly. "This is great!" He said, smiling at his friends.

"Are we ready to go?" He said, offering his hand to Alona.

They gathered up their lights and slowly made their way down the corridor following Georgi and Alona with Aussie flying above them.

"Try not to touch anything, we don't need any more rat traps going off now do we!" Aussie commanded pleased that everything was going great so far.as they reached the doorway opening they all stopped, Georgi stood in the doorway and with his arm outstretched leaned into the room trying to put the light as far as he could in the room without stepping in.

"Looks okay to me!" He said wanting to enter and have a good look around.

"Wait! Hand me a light, and I'll fly with it," Aussie declared, approaching Freddie to borrow the light. He grasped it in his talons and slowly flew into the room. After travelling a short distance, he halted.

"Come up here. It's alright so far, but we need more light!" Aussie called out, as they inched closer to where he was hovering. Freddie had now picked up the light that Aussie had left behind in the corridor and followed behind Mikey.

"Aussie please fly around the edge of the room and then as near as you can guess to the centre, so we can get a better view with all the lights."

The group watched with anticipation as Aussie cautiously flew around the room. When he arrived at the corner opposite them, they spotted another sealed door, identical to the one they had entered through.

"Maybe it's through that door?" Freddie asked, hoping like everyone else to find something.

"According to the map, that door likely leads to the passage where Siruss is located. So, we don't want to open that door, do we?" Georgi reasoned, cautioning against opening the door.

The group placed the lights at strategic locations around the room, and the environment gradually became more visible. "There's something over there in the back!" Alona exclaimed. Aussie cautiously retraced his steps, and all of a sudden, an incredible sight appeared before them. In front of them was a stone pedestal, and at the centre of it rested a smaller stone plinth. Everyone fell silent for a moment, awestruck by the sight of the smaller plinth.

"Is that it?" Squealed Alona, not completely sure that this was what they were looking for.

"It's amazing!" Remarked Freddie slightly stunned.

"I think that's really it!" Mikey answered gleefully.

"It must be it!" Stated Georgi as they all continued to stare at this wonder before them.

"The Crown of Hairies, we found the Crown! Guys, do you realize what this means?" Aussie checked in as they realised their quest had been achieved!

"I think it means we found the Crown!" Aussie and Freddie said sarcastically.

"Ha! Ha! Very funny retorted Aussie"

"That means the end of the rat problem, and we can return to the way things were before the rat group made life miserable in Landon!" Georgi exclaimed, a wide grin spreading across his face as he gingerly picked up the Crown. "Be careful, Georgi," Aussie cautioned.

Suddenly, Mikey's warning echoed in their minds as the smaller plinth began sinking into the larger one. They could hear the sound of something hitting the floor, followed by the grinding of rocks against each other. Georgi hastily returned the Crown to its place, hoping that it wasn't too late. For a moment, there was silence. But then, the same eerie sound of grinding rocks resumed.

Then almost from nowhere a voice came, "hello, my beautiful friends!"

"Who said that?" Alona asked, bewildered by the strange sound. But then the voice chimed in, "It was just in time for dinner!" he exclaimed with excitement.

But before he could say anything else he let out a huge groan as though he was in pain.

"Give me the Crown!" He commanded.

Georgi was just about to take the Crown when Mikey screamed.

"No, Georgi, leave it!" Aussie exclaimed. "When you lifted the Crown, it must have triggered something, and now Siruss is trapped in the doorway to the half-closed door. His body is visibly stuck," he explained urgently.

The group froze in fear as they heard Siruss' menacing voice. "Free me!" he screamed. "Or you will be the first one I dine with," he added, sending chills down their spines.

"Okay, so what do you eat?" Alona asked, trying to keep Siruss distracted as the group slowly moved out of his reach.

"Yeah, what then? Feeling much more confident together with his friends. Even though his fear was slowly returning. Before he could answer Georgi added, "you still can't get out of here, we had to use special equipment to come to this place!"

"I know, Freddie. We can't let him loose," Georgi whispered back. "We need to find a way to trap him for good and make sure he can't harm anyone again."

"What if we could take you to the Valley and you could live free?" Georgi continued while trying to answer his friends also.

"And how do you propose to get me there"?" I know it's quite far from here. If my memory serves me correctly?" Siruss queried.

"You're thinking of using Pete!" Of course, great idea!" Interrupted Aussie now understanding Georgi's plan.

"You let Aussie fly you out and fetch our pelican friend and he will carry you down below to freedom."

"And what's to stop him eating me?" He said wanting to know more.

But you are too big for him to eat, and he only eats fish, his every word filled with hope.

"And what's to stop you trapping me in here again when I go to your Pelican friend?" Questioned Siruss wanting to ensure he wasn't about to be tricked.

"Because I will go with you!" Alona quickly answered.

No sooner than she had finished speaking, Georgi asked her what she was doing. "Somebody must guarantee our part and you guys all need to get back with the Crown!"

"Okay as long as you will ensure I arrive there in one piece?" said Siruss. "They are not going to do anything that will endanger me," replied Alona. "Great then the owl needs to go and fetch your pelican friend, " stated Siruss. Georgi nodded and whispered to Aussie some last minute instructions and then spoke aloud and said, "Okay Aussie, go and explain to Professor Badger that we are all okay and fetch Pete to take Siruss to Rat Valley." Although Aussie knew, Georgi had made up the Rat Valley name to fool Siruss.

CHAPTER TWELVE

FREEDOM FOR SIRUSS?

"Ooo, Rat Valley sounds like a feast! Wait a minute, I hope this isn't some kind of trick? Siruss asked. "It's no trick," Georgi answered. "Professor Badger knows we are all down here and if he doesn't hear from us shortly, he will start to dig us out and that will mean lots of badgers down here, maybe even the whole Badger Brigade!" Georgi said, eager to get Siruss out of there.

"I definitely don't want that," said Siruss, looking worried as he beckoned Aussie to go get Pete. Aussie nervously squeezed past the still trapped Siruss telling everyone that he would fly as quickly as he could. "Breathe in a bit Siruss so I can get past." Aussie asked nervously. Siruss pulled in his belly and Aussie disappeared into the tunnels behind Siruss. "Please hurry" came the nervous chorus from his friends, but Aussie had already flown through the tunnel.

Siruss had already realised that this way was his only chance of getting safely out of these tunnels and Georgi and his friends sensed this. Aussie flew the short distance to the cliff top where Professor Badger and the Badger Brigade were patiently waiting. He quickly relayed Georgi's plan to the Professor who immediately dispatched a member of the Badger Brigade to run the short distance to the lake and get Pete Pelican. While they were waiting the Professor instructed Aussie on what he needed to do when he returned to the tunnels. This shocked Aussie because he thought that his part was already complete, and he didn't expect to have to return to the tunnels while Siruss was still there. "No problem, Professor, anything to help the guys down there," he said anxiously.

Very quickly Pete arrived wanting to help. "What do you need me to do, how are the guys trapped? He asked, eager to support his friends. Aussie quickly explained the situation with Siruss and what they needed him to do. "Yuk, a snake in my mouth, utterly disgusting! Pete exclaimed. "But if it helps save my friends then of course I'll do it." At that point Professor Badger took Pete to one side for some last minute instructions and Aussie heard the Professor saying to Pete that he would inform Aussie later.

"Okay Professor, message received and understood, Aussie let's get going, the sooner we get this done the sooner things get back to normal and have something to eat and some fun!" Pete said eagerly. "Fantastic, please follow me Pete," came Aussie's nervous reply.

"Aussie you have nothing to worry about, soon it will be over and Siruss will bother us no more," Pete stated, confident in the Professor's plan. "Everything is under control," he added.

Pete followed Aussie down to the tunnel entrance and waited outside as Aussie nervously entered the tunnel. "Stay positive Aussie, all will be great, just remember that you're not the one who has to put Siruss in your mouth!" Said Pete, pointing out his predicament. "I'll be fine," Aussie said, as he entered the tunnel.

"Aussie is back!" Freddie shouted. "He better have brought that Pelican friend of yours with him," scowled Siruss, sensing his time in captivity was almost at an end. "Guys, Pete is waiting, you can open the door now, "said Aussie. "First you give me the girl," said Siruss referring to his hostage, Alona. Without hesitation for her own safety Alona made her way towards Siruss. "Make sure those spikes are down," ordered Siruss, making sure he didn't get injured as he slowly moved to wrap his body around Alona. "Not too hard Siruss," Georgi commanded. "Remember the badgers are waiting above, ready to dig if there is any problem," added Aussie.

Okay you can remove the crown now," instructed Siruss with Alona firmly in his grasp. "Are you okay Alona," Georgi asked, determined not to open the door until he knew Alona was safe. "Yes, it is fine, not too tight, let's get this over with," answered Alona wishing to get Siruss out of there. Georgi slowly lifted the crown and the door slowly creaked as it started to open, grinding until Siruss was free. Siruss slowly turned and moved through the door, tasting the air with his tongue to be certain there were no badgers nearby. Aussie had already moved to the tunnel exit but when he got there Pete was nowhere to be seen. "Pete where are you," he shouted, alarmed that his friend was not there. Siruss then appeared at the exit, "what's going on owl," he scowled. "This better not be some kind of trick, or I will crush your friend," said Siruss as he started to tighten his grip on Alona.

"It's no trick, just wait a few seconds while I find him," he said, extremely worried and wondering what the Professor had planned. At that moment Pete appeared, "sorry but I cannot hover for very long and I want to save my energy for carrying you," Pete exclaimed, hoping to resolve this quickly and worried that he couldn't see Alona in the dark tunnel.

"Where is Alona, is she okay, I can't see her?" Pete demanded.

"I'm fine," Alona shouted from inside the darkness. "Let's take Siruss out of here and get this over with," she continued. "Okay

Siruss, slowly get into my throat pouch and spread your weight onto my back and we'll get you out of here", Pete ordered.

Siruss slowly inched out of the cave resting his head and upper body on Pete's bill and started to lower his body into Pete's enormous throat pouch. Alona quickly became visible with Siruss's tail wrapped around her, gripping her to prevent any escape. With most of his weight in Pete's pouch, Siruss moved Alona and the tail end of his body onto Pete's body so that Alona was now on Pete's back. "Let's get going," shouted Siruss triumphantly. "I'm free, I'm free, at long last, I'm free" Siruss said gleefully as Pete moved away from the cave tunnel and began their journey to transfer Siruss and free Alona.

Meanwhile back at the caves Georgi, Mikey, Freddie had arrived back at the Botmarine. "Am I glad to see you guys, it is very scary being here alone in the dark" Andre said as the darkness disappeared as the glow flies lit up the cavern. "Where are Alona and Aussie?" Andre continued. Georgi and Freddie explained about Siruss, Alona, Aussie, and Pete as he clutched the Crown of Hairies. Mikey with the glow flies entered the Botmarine and were eager for news about Alona, Pete, Aussie and Siruss but mainly, they needed to know that Alona was safe. Georgi asked Andre if he could get them back to the lakeside as quickly as possible because he can swim faster than the Botmobile.

Georgi signalled to Mikey that the hatch was sealed, and Mikey started their slow descent on Andre's back. The cave walls were now brightly illuminated as the glow flies grouped together into a ball shape near the centre of the Botmarine. As they reached the tunnel to the lake Andre leaned forward to keep the Botmarine on his back as he accelerated into the tunnel. The darkness surrounding them quickly faded as they moved through the tunnel towards the lake and daylight appeared in front of them. Andre manoeuvred towards the surface as Mikey gave the order to move the levers to empty the water out so that they could surface without all the extra weight from the water they used to submerge.

It was so quiet with everyone thinking about their friends and wondering how everything was working out. As they reached the surface Georgi started to speak but stopped before any words were spoken. "I was going to ask Aussie to fly ahead and bring the Professor," Georgi said, remembering that Aussie was keeping a watchful eye on Alona. "I do hope they are all okay", he said, as he smiled. "I'm sure they will all be okay," said Mikey. "Pete will look after them," he added.

Pete was flying away from the mountain with Siruss who still had Alona, tightly constricted on his back. Pete was flying as fast as he could whilst making sure Alona was safe and comfortable. He flew over forests and a river trying to make sure to drop Siruss as far from Landon as possible. From his beak he heard a muffling, Pete Opened his beak to let Siruss Speak. "Set me down, we have been flying for long enough now!" Hissed Siruss, clearly frustrated. "Once we get to the edge of the forest, I will set you down and we can all be on our way" Mumbled Pete with a mouthful of Siruss. "Well don't hang about, I'm not comfy in here, we would hate for your little friend to become uncomfortable!" Snapped Siruss.

Once the Forest edge appeared, Pete spotted a clearing where he could slow down and land safely. As he slowly descended, he arched the back of his wings to slow down their descent. "Prepare for a bumpy landing" he shouted. Pete knew that this landing would be difficult with the extra weight of a full grown snake in his bill and the trick that he had up his sleeve that he was clutching tightly in one of his feet. Pete bounced across the ground, hopping but trying to use his clenched foot to steady the landing.

As he eventually came to a stop Siruss remarked, "That was a pretty rough landing" and then slithered out of Pete's beak and onto the clearing floor.

"You should try landing with a mouth full of snake!" Pete answered, clearly miffed at Siruss's comments. "You are free, now release Alona and we shall be on our way!" Demanded Pete.

Siruss glared at Pete saying, "Watch your tongue you feathered fool!"

"Please let me go, I agreed to come of my own free will" Pleaded Alona hoping to be free of Siruss's grip and put this ordeal behind her.

"Well, I do like hedgehogs, but a deal is a deal" mused Sirus, excited at his newfound freedom and believing his next meal will soon be rats.

With a huge sigh of relief Alona said "Thank you Siruss" as he loosened his grip and began to slither away.

"Be gone before I change my mind" Siruss hissed before slithering away.

Alona started sobbing more from relief and happiness than anything else, being bound by that snake, not knowing for how long or how it would end took its toll.

Pete tried to comfort Alona by saying "I hope you're ok, it's an extremely brave thing that you've done". Alona nodded in agreement while wiping her eyes, "I bet I know what would cheer you up" stated Pete. "Wh wh what would that be?" queried Alona, still sobbing. "I say you hop on my back, we get out of here and go find our friends" Pete replied enthusiastically.

Before he could finish, Alona jumped onto Pete's back with a big smile on her face and took a good handful of his feathers, so she would remain secure. "That sounds fantastic, let's go!" Alona said, now making herself comfortable on Pete's back. With that Pete stretched out his wings and started flapping, rising high into the sky above the clearing.

Further and further with each flap, as he turned to fly in almost the same direction as they could see Siruss heading, when he saw Aussie hurriedly flying towards them.

As Aussie got closer, he said, "do you know that you are flying the wrong way?"

"The Mission isn't over yet Aussie, jump on my back and speak quietly! Pete commanded, eager to finish the last part of the mission.

Aussie flew onto Pete's back and hugged Alona, who was still clinging onto Pete's Feathers.

"I am so happy to see you, are you okay?" Aussie asked wanting to be reassured that everything is fine with his friend.

"I'm great now Siruss has gone, just trying to stay on Pete's back!" She answered with a smile, pleased that all of this would soon be over.

"We'll be on our way back in just a few minutes, only the last thing to do for Professor Badger" he stated.

"There we should be far enough ahead of Siruss now!" He added, as he opened his left foot and released a small item of clothing from his clenched foot. He then started to turn homewards, "What was that?" Asked Aussie, who with Alona was looking very confused.

"Professor Badger had a great idea, of taking an item of rat clothing with me. Snakes use smell using their tongues, so the Professor thought that it was necessary for Siruss to be able to smell a rat, as they say. I dropped it further away to lure him in that direction. Also, we flew over a river to try and keep him on this side of the river, as far away from us as possible." Explained Pete who was now flying towards Landon.

"That's brilliant" stated Aussie, "I can't wait to get home now and see our friends!" Alona replied, having had a rough day.

"We'll soon be back soon" declared Pete, wondering if their friends were safely back from their amazing adventure.

Meanwhile back on the Botmarine, the guys were getting close to land. They could see a lot of their friends and neighbours gathering around the Botmarine landing site. People were standing and cheering louder the closer they got to the land.

Georgi stood with the crown and thrust it into the air to a chorus of louder cheers. As he held the crown, Freddie commented "I don't think raising the crown was such a good idea, with the rats not so far away!".

"These animals here already know about the crown so I'm sure that the rats will" he answered. "I think I just saw some rats jumping into the lake on the other side," Freddie added. "Don't worry, my friends will take care of them" Andre Answered as he began walking slowly out of the lake.

"There are badger battalion soldiers here also" Andre added, as he gently lowered his body at the front so that the Botmarine slid onto the grass in front of him. "Hold tight" he said as he gave the Botmarine a push, so it landed on the ground below as it cleared his head. "All ashore that's going ashore!" he continued with a sigh of relief that he had brought his friends safely back, well almost anyway.

Now that they were back on land Mikey quickly opened the hatch and everyone jumped out of the Botmarine. Georgie quickly ran to one of the badger brigades, "is there any word on our friends, Alona, Aussie and Pete?" he asked.

"No! We have not heard anything!" replied the guard. "Thanks anyway," Georgi answered. Georgi could feel his eyes filling with tears. He told himself that he wasn't going to get upset but it was too extremely difficult as the one thought that kept appearing in his mind "Why did he take these friends on such a dangerous mission?"

Just then the guys heard shouting, but they looked around and couldn't see anything. As the shouting became louder someone pointed to the sky. "What can it be now?" Georgi thought, having already been through more than enough today. But as he looked up Freddie said, "It's Pete, It's Pete, They are back"! As the guys heard Alona and Aussie's voices the day just got better and better.

"They are back, and they are okay, How wonderful!" Georgi shouted in excitement.

Pete glided in and made his trademark stuttering landing and came to a halt next to his friends. "You are all okay…we are all so glad to see you back safely, we didn't know what to expect with that devious serpent!"

Georgi said, clearly relieved to see his friends. "Alona, you can let go now, we've landed, and we are safe!" Pete said, wanting Alona to let go.

"Sorry Pete", replied Alona, as she let go of Pete's feathers, and slid down Pete's wing which was angled towards the ground. As she landed her friends quickly ran to her for hugs.

Meanwhile back at the lake many animals had gathered to greet our heroes on their return. As the Botmarine arrived at the side of the lake the crowd cheered as Andre tilted forward and the Botmarine gently slid from Andre's back and into the water. Andre moved to the rear of the Botmarine as Mikey opened the hatch and Mikey and his friends climbed out. Andre quickly pushed the Botmarine and as soon as it slid on the land the guys immediately jumped to the ground and their gaze was drawn to the distant figures at the cliff edge, near where Pete collected Siruss at the tunnel entrance. They were all thinking the same thing, "where were their friends and were they okay?

Georgi held the crown of Hairies in the air to rapturous cheers from the growing crowd, animals were still streaming towards them and swelling the crowd. Within a few minutes Professor Badger arrived with the Badger Brigade, his face was beaming as he saw the crown glimmering in the sunshine. "Well done guys! Hopefully now we can end all this trouble that we have been having", he continued as the crowd cheered yet again.

Just then a voice was heard from above, "hey guys we are okay we are back!" Aussie shouted triumphantly. "I flew ahead to tell you the great news! Siruss is far away, Pete and Alona are fine and will be with you shortly!"

This brought an even louder cheer from the crowd and the guys as Aussie landed, panting heavily, almost breathless from his rush to tell them the good news.

In the distance they could now clearly see Pete quickly flying towards them, his big gleaming smile visible even from a distance.

"Everyone please move back" Professor Badger ordered, wanting to ensure that Pete could land safely, especially considering Pete's history of bad landings. But he needn't have worried as Pete made a series of quick flaps and then landed right beside the guys.

The crowd cheered yet again as Pete tipped his wing to the floor to allow Alona to join the guys.

Alona gratefully slid down the pelican's wing and into the arms of her waiting friends. "Boy am I so glad to see you guys!" She said as she looked at her friends, "we are all together again at last!"

"It's great to see you safe and well too Alona!" answered Georgi. "We have all been wondering what was happening with you, Pete and Aussie, since you left, but now everything is just great!" added Mikey.

Pete made his way over to the Professor and told him that his plan worked perfectly but he also advised him of another worry. "When I was landing, I noticed thousands of rats erecting what looked like a massive army camp!" Pete said, then pointing to the huge camp in the distance.

"I hope it is not more trouble, " answered Professor Badger, "thanks Pete I'll take some of the Badger Brigade and find out what is happening. The Professor ordered some of the soldiers to take Georgi and friends to safety and guard the Crown of Hairies as he quickly made his way to the camp.

The guys decided to go to Georgi's Grandma's as they deserved some pie and tea after all that they had been through. When they arrived at Grandma's, Georgi's radiating smile couldn't hide from his Grandma that something really big, and amazing had happened. When he showed his Grandma the Crown of Hairies she started crying tears of happiness, so very proud of what her grandson and his friends had achieved, there were hugs all round for Georgi and his friends.

As the gang was enjoying their well earned tea and cherry pie Professor Badger returned.

"Is everything okay Professor," Georgi asked, eager to know what was occurring.

"For once Georgi everything is just Perfect! The professor stated triumphantly.

"So, what is that nearby campsite for?" Georgi asked, eager for news.

"It's the rats, their spies had informed them that we had located the Crown of Hairies and they have come here to show their gratitude, pay their respects, reclaim their crown and ensure it was returned to its rightful owners!" The Professor answered in a relieved tone.

"I told them that the Crown will be returned at a festival tomorrow, in your honour!"

The following day the festival grounds quickly filled with animals of all shapes and sizes. There were rabbits, foxes, mice, squirrels, and even a large variety of birds. The air was filled with the sound of chatter and laughter as the array of different animals mingled together, all the animals wanted to celebrate living together in peace and harmony eagerly awaiting the presentation of the Crown of Hairies to the rat king which should ensure tranquillity. This would not only return the crown but celebrate their friendship and community. The animals came from all over to enjoy the fun, music and dancing, games, and rides, and of course, plenty of food to eat.

Georgi's Grandma had made her famous cherry pie, and she was bringing it to the festival to share with everyone. The animals were so excited to try Grandma's pie. They had all heard stories about how delicious it was, and they couldn't wait to get a taste.

When Grandma arrived at the festival, she was greeted by a crowd of animals. They all wanted a piece of her pie, and she was happy to share. They all agreed that Grandma's pie was the best they had ever tasted.

Georgi and his friends stood at the front of the stage, admiring the Crown displayed on the podium in front of them. They were all dressed in their finest attire, feeling both proud and nervous at the same time.

Professor Badger stood up. "Ladies and gentlemen," he began, his voice booming over the crowd, "it is my great pleasure to honour Pete the pelican for his quick thinking and decisive action in saving the crown. Pete, you will always be welcome in Landon for as long as you want to stay here." Pete bowed as everyone present clapped and cheered for their newest addition to Landon.

"Without further ado I would like to ask Georgi to come forward and present the Crown of Hairies to the rat king and return an ancient artefact that has been finally found!"

The crowd erupted into cheers and applause as Professor Badger carefully removed the cover revealing the shimmering Crown that had been cleaned and polished.

The rat king sat upon his throne, looking out over the crowd with pride. "Thank you, Georgi and Friends, Professor Badger plus all the animals of Landon," he said, his voice echoing across the festival grounds. "It is an honour to accept this magnificent Crown on behalf of all the rats of Landon."

As the ceremony continued, Georgi and his friends watched anxiously from the edge of the crowd. Something didn't feel right and they knew that the rebel rats were still out there somewhere, waiting for the perfect moment to strike.

Suddenly, there was a big commotion at the back of the crowd. Georgi turned just in time to see a group of rebel rats making their way towards the front of the stage, their eyes fixed greedily on the Crown of Hairies.

"We've got to stop them!" Alona cried, taking off after the rebels.

Georgi and Mikey followed close behind, weaving through the crowd with determination. They could hear the sounds of the rats' rapid footsteps powering the car in the distance, growing louder and louder with each passing moment.

When they reached the front of the stage, they found the rebel rats were already there, making a mad dash for the Crown. Georgi and his friends sprang into action, diving towards the rebels with all their might.

"We won't let you get away with this!" Georgi shouted, trying to grab the Crown from the rebel rats' grasp.

But it was too late. The rebels had already grabbed the Crown and jumped into their car to speed away, the Crown of Hairies clutched tightly in their paws.

Georgi and his friends looked on in despair as the rebel rats disappeared into the distance. "What are we going to do now?" Mikey asked, his voice filled with worry.

But no sooner than the words had left his mouth, Pete the pelican appeared overhead. "Not so fast, rebels!" he cried, swooping down towards the speeding car, he had filled his enormous bill to the brim with water.

In one swift movement, he emptied his load onto the rebels, dousing them in a massive deluge of water. The car crashed to a halt, and the wet and soggy rebels were now dazed and lying in a giant puddle. Professor Badger and his Badger Brigade were quickly on the scene.

"I'll take that, thank you!" Professor Badger said sarcastically as he picked up the crown.

The Badger Brigade and some soldiers from rat city took the rebel rats to the rat city camp to be locked up.

Georgi and his friends looked on with pride as the Crown of Hairies was returned to the rat king. They knew that Pete had saved the day again, and that their bravery had made a difference. The Professor summoned Georgi and his friends to the stage.

"You three have shown great bravery today," the Professor said. "You have risked your lives to protect the Crown of Hairies, and I am proud of you. As a reward, I hereby declare you to be honorary members of the Badger Brigade!"

Georgi, Mikey, and Alona cheered as the Professor pinned a badge on Pete and on each of their chests. They had saved the day, and they were now official members of the Badger Brigade!

The Professor then turned to the crowd. "Citizens of Rat City!" he called out. "I present to you our new heroes, Georgi, Pete, Mikey, Alona, Freddie and Aussie! They have risked their lives to protect our city, and they deserve our thanks!"

The crowd erupted into cheers as they all took a bow. They had saved the day, and they were now heroes!

After the presentation Georgi and his friends sat together, basking in the warm glow of their success. They knew that they had learned an important lesson about the power of teamwork and the importance of standing up for what is right.

As the festival drew to a close, they watched the animals of Landon dance and sing together in celebration, they knew that they had made a positive difference, and that the future was bright and promising.

Georgi stood up and said, "Here's to many adventures together!"

The End

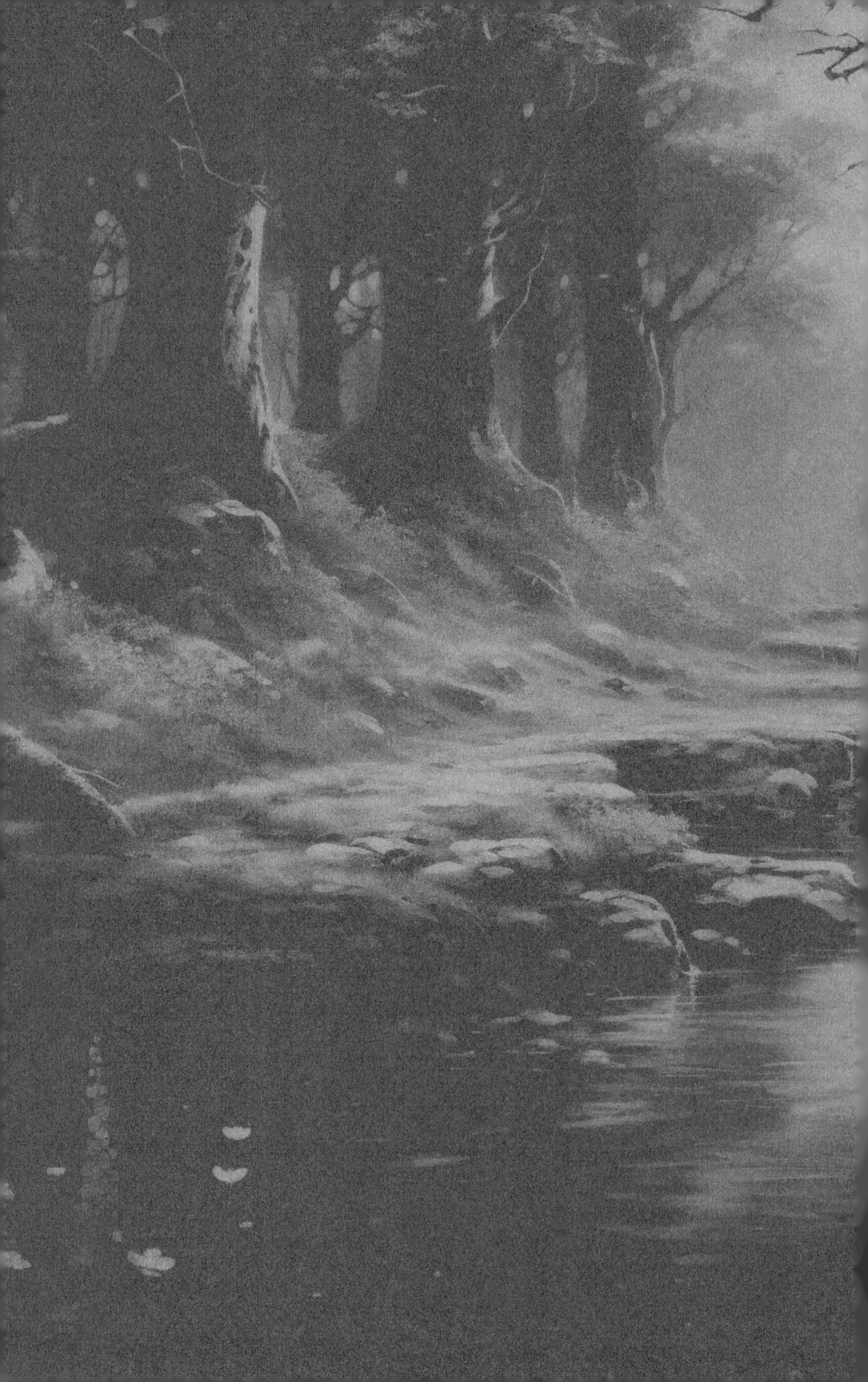

ABOUT THE AUTHOR

Glynn is inspired by his own children and grandchildren, and a love of stories that will make them laugh and learn. I am also a passionate advocate for literacy, and believe that reading is one of the most important gifts that a parent can give their child.

Glynn started writing this children's book over 8 years ago, working on the book in his spare time, and now, it has finally been published.

I hope that my book will encourage children to read and explore the world of their own imagination.

When I'm not writing, like all parents and grandparents, I enjoy spending time with my family and am always up for playing games and having fun. As a loving and supportive father and grandfather, my family is very important to me, and I cherish the time that I get to spend with them.

This book is dedicated to my children, grandchildren who I have always loved to tell stories to. Also it is dedicated to my passion to help all the children of the world develop a love of reading.

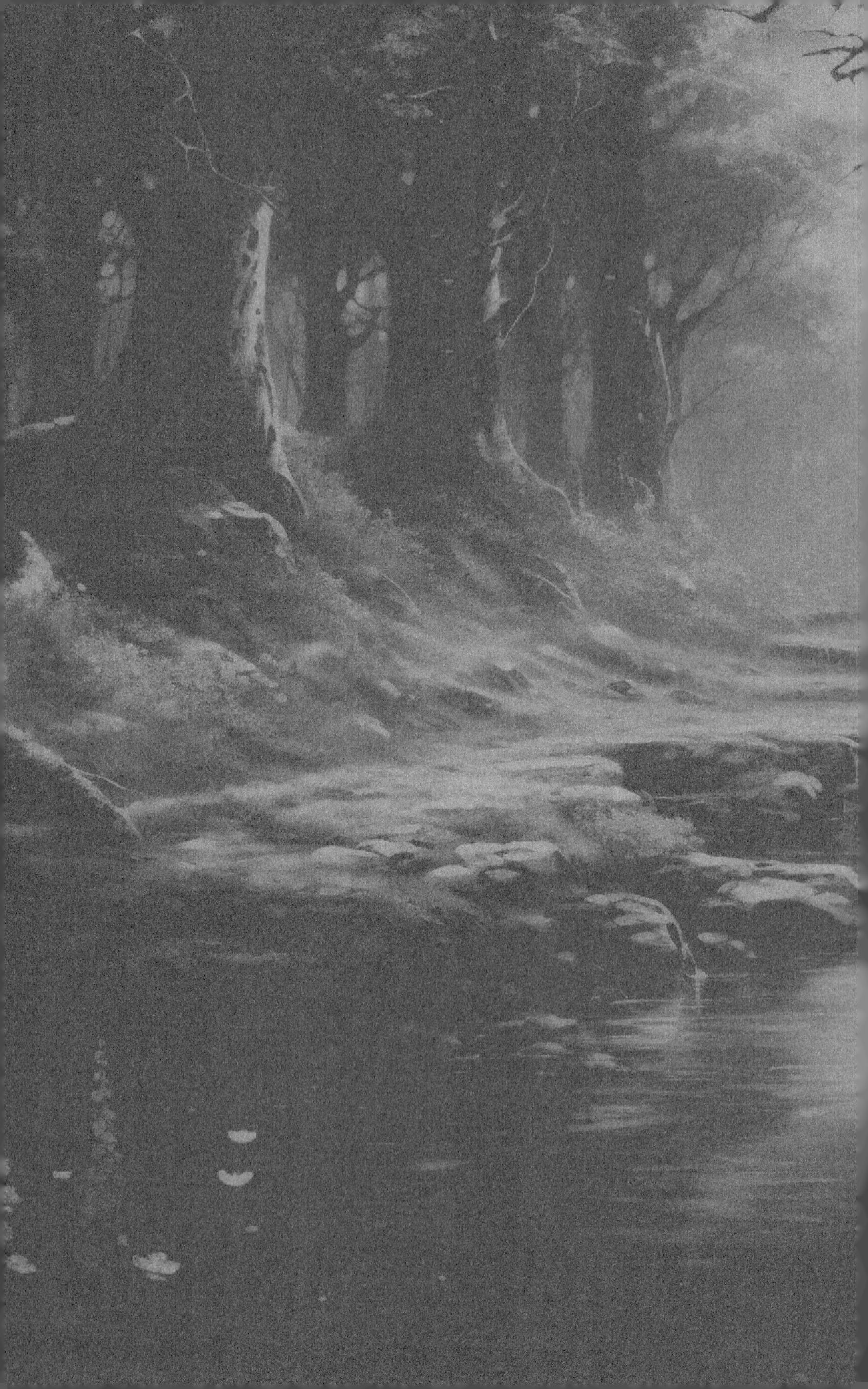

Printed in Great Britain
by Amazon